The Drinks Are on the Kingdom:

The Wedding at Cana and the Kingdom of God

By Pastor Jim Hill

The Drinks Are on the Kingdom
By Pastor Jim Hill

Copyright © 2007 by Jim Hill
The North Clairemont United Methodist Church
4570 Mt. Herbert Avenue
San Diego, California 92117
Printed in the United States of America
ISBN 1-931178-23-2

All rights reserved solely by the author. The author guarantees all contents are original and do not infringe upon the legal rights of any other person or work. No part of this book may be reproduced in any form without the permission of the author. The views expressed in this book are not necessarily those of the publisher.

Most scripture quotations, unless otherwise indicated, are taken from the NIV.

"THE DRINKS ARE ON THE KINGDOM" – p. 3

TABLE OF CONTENTS

Introduction 5
The Story of the Wedding at Cana 9
Chapter 1: How I Got to This Wedding 11
Chapter 2: Life in the Kingdom Is a Party 33
Chapter 3: The Drinks Are on the Kingdom 51
Chapter 4: The Whole Village Was Invited 69
Chapter 5: The Best Is Yet to Come 87
Chapter 6: Signs of the Nature and Presence of God 107
Small Group Study Guide Helps 129
Session 1 Guide 139
Session 2 Guide 143
Session 3 Guide 147
Session 4 Guide 151
Session 5 Guide 155
Session 6 Guide 159
Bibliography 163
About the Author 164

"THE DRINKS ARE ON THE KINGDOM" – p. 4

"THE DRINKS ARE ON THE KINGDOM" – p. 5

INTRODUCTION

In one way, this book is a study of the wedding at Cana as recorded in John chapter 2, especially, but not solely, focusing on the actions of Jesus. I will dwell on five particular points which I see this passage teach us. There are other points one could see in this passage, and valuable ones too, but these are the ones that God has impressed upon me for this study.

As you will see in the first chapter, I was drawn to this piece of scripture at this time by a lecture I heard at the National Pastor's Convention in February of 2006. Then I began to reflect upon this passage more, and these five themes were strongly impressed upon me. Yet there is one overriding theme. It is expressed in the title: The Drinks Are on the Kingdom.

Since Jesus was the one who made the wine, and since we Christians are everywhere told that we are to be and do like Jesus, then it should follow that whatever is meant by Jesus making that wine is what we also are to do. There is, again, more than one thing meant by his actions in making that wine, but one thing that is clear is that it was He who took the initiative to solve a problem, to make the party a success, to bring joy. Following his example then, it is we who are his followers who are to do likewise. If the "drinks" were "on" Jesus, and we are his followers, ones who follow in his footsteps, then "the drinks" should be on us! Then we should be the ones responsible to take the initiative to make life different for others. Does that not follow?

There are other themes here, and they are meaningful and important and worthy of their own reflection. One or more of these other themes may be what is most critical for you at this point in your life, and that will be fine. However, throughout this study, bear in mind that one important theme in our Christian life is that somehow the initiative is supposed to be on us who are in Christ, and periodically ask yourself what that must mean for you in your circumstances.

Ask yourself some of these questions: Is that so? Why is that so? How can that be so? What should that lead to? What will I allow that to lead to in my own life?

This book will read well just as a study by itself, but it is also designed for small group study. There are meeting suggestions and discussion questions for each chapter at the back of this book. Your group and leader should make what adjustments you need to make it work best for you.

"THE DRINKS ARE ON THE KINGDOM" – p. 7

I hope you enjoy reading this slender volume. I hope that you are delighted by much of it, encouraged by much of it and challenged by much of it. I hope it gives you a passion to be more like Jesus.

Good luck. God bless you. And go to now.

Pastor Jim Hill
San Diego, California
December, 2006

"THE DRINKS ARE ON THE KINGDOM" – p. 8

"THE DRINKS ARE ON THE KINGDOM" – p. 9

THE STORY OF THE WEDDING AT CANA

On the third day a wedding took place at Cana in Galilee. Jesus' mother was there, and Jesus and his disciples had also been invited to the wedding. When the wine was gone, Jesus' mother said to him, "They have no more wine."

"Dear woman, why do you involve me?" Jesus replied. 'My time has not yet come."

His mother said to the servants, "Do whatever he tells you."

Nearby stood six stone water jars, the kind used by the Jews for ceremonial washing, each holding from twenty to thirty gallons.

Jesus said to the servants, "Fill the jars with water"; so they filled them to the brim.

Then he told them, "Now draw some out and take it to the master of the banquet."

They did so, and the master of the banquet tasted the water that had been turned into wine. He did not realize where it had come from, though the servants who had drawn the water knew. Then he called the bridegroom aside and said, "Everyone brings out the choice wine first

"THE DRINKS ARE ON THE KINGDOM" – p. 10

and then the cheaper wine after the guests have had too much to drink; but you have saved the best till now."

This, the first of his miraculous signs, Jesus performed in Cana in Galilee. He thus revealed his glory, and his disciples put their faith in him.

- John 2:1-11

"THE DRINKS ARE ON THE KINGDOM" – p. 11

CHAPTER 1: HOW I GOT TO THIS WEDDING

I Didn't Want to Go

I am not good about taking time off for study leave. It is my fault, no one else's, and Russ Loehr, current chair of SPRC, our personnel committee, was trying to help me out. Months ahead of time he signed me up to go to the National Pastors' Conference in February, with my approval, mind you. If you ask someone well enough in advance, you greatly improve the odds that they will agree, since they cannot see how busy their schedule will be that far in advance. It is held in San Diego, my hometown, so there is no travel expense. He even suggested that I take a day or two at the Town and Country Hotel to make it more of a get-a-way, but that was too bold for me. I stayed home, but I went.

The first two days I hated it. I went to a pre-conference seminar on new ways to "do" church. All the presenters were young. I thought most of them were awfully full of themselves, and not nearly as clever as they said they were. I did not mind the things they recommended to try, for some settings, after all, in each age we keep doing things in new ways to communicate, but I thought the theology they used to justify it was dangerously

"THE DRINKS ARE ON THE KINGDOM" – p. 12

sloppy and sure to lead to problems they apparently did not see. I suspect that they all came from very conservative church backgrounds, and to them the evident need was to pry people loose from the past ("We've never done it that way before."), but I come from a more "modern" denomination, and we sometimes have to worry about our leaders trying to make golden calves. Of course, I am sure that my jealousy (because they each had a book published and I only had an article or two) did not affect my judgment.

Then I heard a nationally known speaker, whom I admire for his passion and whom I have read some, speak much too broadly on issues with which he did not display nearly enough breadth of knowledge or reflection to justify his very sweeping and harshly judgmental positions, especially since they tended to differ from mine. (We tend to enjoy judgmentalism only when we agree with the judgments.) The next day I had to go to a Board of Evangelism meeting in Pasadena, and I missed the next speaker, whom I had really wanted to hear. I was getting really bummed out on this conference, walking about muttering things under my breath, looking for someone to speak with only to have a place to complain, and so on.

"THE DRINKS ARE ON THE KINGDOM" – p. 13

Then I began to hear some great preachers. Anne Graham Lotz was the first one I heard, and I thought, "Boy, when I grow up, I want to do Bible studies like her." John Ortberg, David Anderson, and Steve Chalke were others, and I was humbled by their skill. I said, "Oh yes. Let me sit at the feet of the masters and learn." I would doubtless have stolen more of their illustrations to use in sermons right away except that right after this conference, I was working on a series on life in community, and I was already stealing heavily from Rick Warren for that. However, one message really stood out for me. Of course I enjoyed hearing it. I thought he proclaimed one truth that was dear to me, but he proclaimed another that I decided ought to be dear to me, and then as I looked at the passage of scripture upon which his message was based I saw a couple of other pretty good things too.

In some form I have "given" this message six or seven times already, in casual conversations, and I am still jazzed each time I give it. I think it is sound, it is Biblical, it is fun, it is challenging, and it is helpful. I hope you find it fun. I am okay if you find it challenging. I hope you catch the same virus of joy and enthusiasm to bring its points to life that I have.

"THE DRINKS ARE ON THE KINGDOM" – p. 14

I am going to tell you a story. It is Steve Chalke's story, although I may have jiggered it a little in the retelling. He is a British Baptist who spoke at this Conference. It will serve as an introduction to this little book. If I did no more than tell this story, it would be a good start. It is a good story. I will, however, also make a note of five points which I see in the scripture that this book is based on, John 2:1-11, the wedding at Cana. Okay, now here goes the Steve Chalke Story.

The Steve Chalke Story

Steve Chalke said that he was raised a Baptist in Britain. You need to know that the churches in England are not doing very well. (I was in London on a Sunday in 1994. I went to three churches that day. Don't be too surprised; it is sort of my business. The first one was Westminster Abbey. Somewhere during the service, I muttered to myself that if I were an Englishman, I would be an atheist. Just to be fair, the Methodist Central Hall service, to which I went right after the Westminster Abbey service, was not much better.) The overwhelming majority of folks do not go to church in England, but he did. His family did. They lived about a mile and a half from the church they went to, when he was young, and they walked to church. They walked a mile and a half to church for morning service, and then they walked a mile and a half back home. They had lunch, and then they walked a mile and a half back to church for afternoon Bible study, and then they walked a mile and a half back home. They had dinner, and then they walked a mile and a half back to church for evening service, and then they walked a mile and a half back home. Now all this time, Steve was in his Sunday best, and his mates were out playing ball, while he was walking back and forth to church. He wanted to play ball, but he went to church.

Realize also that in his church everything was either *compulsory* or *forbidden*. There was very little that was optional, or in between. You either had to do it, or you couldn't do it. And there were a lot of things you could not do. The boys in his youth group had a little chant that went like this: "We don't smoke and we don't chew, and we don't go with girls that do." All the things that you ever heard that the church said you could not do? Well, they couldn't do them.

Somehow (not very well explained), Steve became a Christian. In fact he felt a call into ministry. He went off to college and then to seminary, and then he got a job at a church. This church was a mega-church, for England. Remember that the church, on the whole, does not do very well in England, and this church had a thousand members. He got a job as an assistant at a thousand member Baptist church somewhere in the suburbs of London. Of course, in this church too, everything was pretty much either compulsory or forbidden, and a lot of things were forbidden, drinking, smoking, all the standard things, and maybe a few more. Remember that list of all those things you ever heard that the church said you couldn't do? Well, they couldn't do them either.

After he had been there a while, his wife began to ask him, "Steve, dearest, when are they going to let you preach?" And he would reply, "Well, I don't know. You see I think each staff person has a job description, and I am an assistant pastor, and preaching is not in the assistant pastor's job description." Of course he wanted to preach, but it did not seem likely to happen any time soon.

Then one day, not long after that, the Senior Pastor invited him in to his office. This was a pretty big thing all by itself. He chatted with him a bit, and then he told him that he was going to start a new sermon series. He wanted to talk about the signs of Jesus in the Gospel of John, and

"THE DRINKS ARE ON THE KINGDOM" – p. 17

he wanted Steve to give the first message in the series, to talk about the first miraculous sign.

Well, as you can image, Steve was just delighted with this. Here he was going to get a chance to preach. When he went home that night he told his wife about it. "You know, Pastor Beer," (Peter Beer was the Senior Pastor's name.) has asked me to preach. He's going to do a series on the signs of Jesus in the Gospel of John." "That's great," she said." "This is very important, you know," Steve said to his wife. "There are only about six signs in the gospel of John. Yes, and he wants me to preach on the first one." "That's great," she said again. "By the way, what was the first sign?" [Now let me tell you, when Chalke told this tale at the Conference, everybody was already laughing because they knew what the first sign was. And, if you didn't skip it, you've already read it up front, when you read John 2:1-11.] "What's the first sign?" his wife asked. "I don't know," he answered. "Well," she said, "you ought to find out." "Yes," he said, "Yes, I'll have to find out."

Well, Chalke found out. The first sign in the Gospel of John is the one recorded in John 2:1-11. It consists of turning water into wine, turning 160 to 180

"THE DRINKS ARE ON THE KINGDOM" – p. 18

gallons of water into wine. And this was at a church that thought abstinence ought to be in the Apostles Creed. Now he knew why Senior Pastor Peter Beer had asked him to preach the first sermon.

Steve did his homework. He read and studied and prayed, and then the day to preach came. He got up in the pulpit and read the passage you have already read. Then he began to expound the passage. "What can you do," he asked, "about this text? What can you conclude from what Jesus did? Jesus made 180 gallons of wine for a bunch of people who had already had too much too drink! That's why they were out of wine. They had already drunk it all! So what can you say about a text where Jesus made 180 gallons of wine for a bunch of people who had already had too much to drink? (Pause.) The drinks are on the kingdom!" There was absolute silence.

He thought maybe they hadn't heard him so he more or less repeated himself. "What can you say about a text where Jesus made 180 gallons of wine for a bunch of folks who had already had too much to drink? Life in the Kingdom is a party, and the drinks are on the kingdom!" Still, no one moved a muscle. But the service came to an end.

"THE DRINKS ARE ON THE KINGDOM" – p. 19

Then the time came for him to greet the parishioners after the service. One man who was an elder in the church came through the line. He was well into his eighties, and his name was Harry Cork. (All these names are true, according to Chalke. The names have not been changed to protect anyone.) Harry Cork came up to Steve with a bit of a frown, pursed his lips a bit, and said, "This won't do. This just won't do."

"I know, Harry," said Steve Chalke, "I know. I wanted to preach a better sermon. I wanted to preach one about all the things we are against, but what could I do with the text I had?"

"I know," said Harry Cork. Then, nodding towards the Senior Pastor Peter Beer, he said, "It's his fault."

"No, it's not," said Chalke. For some reason he wanted to protect the Senior Pastor. "No, it's not his fault, and it's not my fault. Do you know whose fault it is?" Chalke asked Harry. "Do you know whose fault it is? It's Jesus' fault. It's Jesus' fault."

"Yes," Harry Cork replied slowly, "Yes. I know. I know," and after a pause Harry said, "It's Jesus' fault … but He was young then."

"THE DRINKS ARE ON THE KINGDOM"

Five Points to Note

So, it's Jesus' fault. John wrote it, but Jesus did it. This text exists because Jesus did it. It's Jesus' fault. And what a great fault it is. Chalke lifted up slightly one theme that I have long championed: that life in the kingdom of God is something like a party. And he lifted up boldly another theme that I had never seen in this passage before: that the "drinks" are on the kingdom, that it is the Christians who are to make life a party. Then as I looked at this passage again, I see five themes that Jesus put there, that I think are important, and that I want to share with you. In this introduction, I'll touch a little upon each theme. Then I'll take a chapter to deal with each one in more depth. Here are those five themes.

Life in the Kingdom Is a Party

Point number one: Life in the kingdom is a party. Is it? But many believe that life in the church means that you never go to a party. Many believe that the essence of being a Christian is to suck lemons and look like a prune. Many believe that Christians are never *for* anything, they are only *against*, and they are against a lot. Isn't it godly to be dour, sour, always serious, always on the lookout for sin? Aren't we to be always on the lookout for someone somewhere that might be having fun so that we can stop him? No! We are not.

Christians should be the happiest people in the world! The word joy is used in the Bible something over a hundred and seventy times, and there are another forty or so uses of joyful, joyfully and joyfulness, and that does not take into account many words of similar meaning. Joy is not a small theme in scripture. "Joy" is what God gives us in place of mourning in Isaiah 61. Joy in the Lord is the source of our strength, we are told in Nehemiah 8:10. It is one of the fruits the Holy Spirit produces in us, as noted in Galatians 5:22. And this theme is splashed throughout the ministry of Jesus.

First of all, we have our text here in John 2. It *was* a wedding feast, you know. Those *were* grand celebrations. And Jesus *did* go, and He did bring his disciples. So going to a party must be okay. And modeling that conduct for your disciples must be okay. Why? Because Jesus did it.

In Matthew 22:2, Jesus compares the kingdom of heaven to a wedding feast prepared by a king. That's not my idea; it's Jesus' fault again.

In Matthew 11:28, Jesus told his hearers to come to him because they would find rest for their souls. Now does rest sound more like dour, sour, sad and mad, or more like joy, and maybe even a bit of a party? He said people should try his way because his way was what really fit their lives.

In John 10:10, Jesus said it is the thief who comes to steal and kill and destroy, and that that was not him! He did not come to take away, but to give. He did not come to kill life, but to give it. He came that we might all have life, and not just a little bit of life, but have life to the full.

So, *life in Christ should be full of joy.*

I like the first question and answer in the Westminster Catechism. The question is: What is the chief end of man? And the answer is: To glorify God and to enjoy Him forever. Now I'm not a Calvinist, so I'm sure there are some things in that Catechism that I would balk at, but I love this part. Most of us think we know about glorifying God. That means doing the do's and not doing the don't's, we think. And that's true, but I suspect that the do's include joy and peace and health in ways we usually don't pay much attention to. Yet I think the real payoff is in the "enjoy Him forever" part. This is key because it is something I think we often miss. We are supposed to enjoy God. You are supposed to enjoy God. Look here, we all

"THE DRINKS ARE ON THE KINGDOM" – p. 23

have ups and downs, and we all start from different places, and God alone is the judge, now, having said all that, still somehow our lives should fundamentally exude, reflect and be full of joy. So much for point number one.

The Drinks Are on the Kingdom

Number two: *The "drinks" are on the kingdom.* Who provided the wine? Who made one hundred and eighty gallons of extra wine? Jesus. It was Jesus. It was Jesus' fault. Now, don't we usually say that we ought to act like Jesus? Do what Jesus did? If so, then doesn't that mean that we who are in Christ should bring the wine?

Look, they mixed two parts of water to three parts of wine. And there was a whole village enjoying this wine. And there are lots of scriptures speaking against habitual drunkenness. That is not the issue here. Wine represents joy. There are also many scriptures which speak of it as an aspect of celebration. It would have been a great embarrassment for the hosts to have run out of wine, and there is more here. Those stone pots for ceremonial washing represented the established way of seeking relationship with God. The perfect number in their culture was seven, and there were six jars. That means the ceremony they represented was imperfect, and Jesus transformed it into something more. But do not lose sight of the simple fact that He made a lot of wine for a party and it was He that did it.

Here is another way to get a handle on what this means. When Peter recognized who Jesus was, Jesus declared, "that you are Rocky [That is what Peter" means, "Rock" or "Rocky."], and on this rock I will build my church, and the gates of Hades will not prevail against it." [Matthew 16:18] Whose gates do not prevail? Whose gates fall down? The gates of Hell. If it is the gates of Hades, that fall down, then who is attacking who? That has got to mean that it is us, the Christians, who are to go out and to take back turf from Satan. We move out. We conquer. And we take responsibility for making life changing things happen.

Look, Jesus also told us, everybody knows something about love. Pagans are nice to one another. Big deal. If you want to be like God, you've got to do more. You love even those who cannot do you any good. You love even those who are harder to love. You reach out to love others because that is what will break down the gates of Hell and begin to draw others into the kingdom life!

"THE DRINKS ARE ON THE KINGDOM" – p. 25

That is the kind of perfection we are called into in Matthew 5:43-48.

It is the Christian who should take the initiative to transform life, to invite others to the party of God, to make life more of a party for others.

The Whole Village Got Invited

Who got invited to this affair at Cana? Here is my point number three: *The whole village was invited.* Everybody was there. Mary was there too, and Jesus, and He brought along his friends, but everybody in the village would have been there.

For us I think that means we try to include everybody too: the person whose theology is wrong, the person who has too much hardware stuck through his body parts, the single parent, the abandoned child, the lonely, the depressed, the ones who do not have their act together yet, the lame, maybe even the guy who tells lame jokes, and so on. Oh, there are places, Matthew 22:11-13 for one, where Jesus speaks of folks who never get the right attitude. Those without the wedding garment can get kicked out of the feast, but first they get invited. We are to invite, reach out to, try to include just about everybody.

"THE DRINKS ARE ON THE KINGDOM" – p. 26

When John, in 3:16, said that God sent his Son into the world to save it, he said that God loved *the whole world*, not just little bitty parts of it. When Jesus, in Matthew 11:28, said folks should come to him because his way worked, He said that *all* should come, "*all* you who are weary and burdened" were his words. They are all invited to church, to the pot-luck, and into the life in the kingdom of God. Jesus, just before He returned to the Godhead, told his disciples to go make disciples from *all* nations. I have noticed that "all" tends to mean "all." When Isaiah foreshadowed Christ's call in chapter 55, he said "Come, *all* you who are thirsty, come to the waters; and you who have no money, come, buy and eat!"

I want messed up people in church! How are they ever going to get to God, if us holy ones keep beating them off with a stick? Jesus said that his Father's house should be a house of prayer for all peoples, not a convenient club for club members. I am not saying that everything everyone does is okay, but I am saying that God loves all people, even the ones who have done messed up things, and, by the way, that is good news for us all, because we have *all* done messed up things! Sometimes we are like fishermen who go out on a lake and expect the fish to clean themselves and filet themselves before they jump into the boat or we won't let them grab a hook. Who are invited to the kingdom of God? *All are invited.*

The Best Is Yet to Come

Number Four: The best was served last. *That means that the best is yet to come.* Always, the best is yet to come. At wedding feasts in Jesus' day, most folks served the good wine first, then, after people had drunk too much to tell very well what they were drinking, then they brought out the cheap stuff. But that was not the case at this party. The steward of the party told the bridegroom that he had saved the best for last. But that illustrates a principle of life in the kingdom of God.

In II Corinthians 3:18, Paul points out that when we are in Christ, we are in glory, but we are not done. We are also going on to glory. We go from one degree of glory on to another. We are not potatoes: "Stick me with a fork, I'm done." We are people, made in the image of God, and continually going on to glory after glory. We should expect to grow in this life of ours. Only idiots and teenagers think they know it all, and frankly, I think, most teenagers really know better than that, they just don't want to let on to mom and dad yet. (So I guess that only leaves idiots.)

This means we should not be smug in our spiritual accomplishments, self-satisfied, proud, and vain. It also means that we can expect life to get even better. It means that we do not *have to settle* for things that we know are not yet right or good or settled in our lives. We can expect more.

Then I think of John Wesley's last words. When he was about to die, he said to someone, "The best of all is this: The best is yet to come." Even after a lifetime of growing in Christ, we can expect still more when we move on to be with Him in eternity. Always, for the Christian, always, the best is yet to come.

Signs Reveal the Glory of God

My last point is about signs. On this occasion, making one hundred and eighty gallons of wine was a sign that revealed something about the nature of God. More generally, we could say, making life a party was the sign which revealed the glory of God. This sign revealed the presence of God, and it also declared something about the nature of God, apparently that He wants his people to have joy.

"THE DRINKS ARE ON THE KINGDOM" – p. 29

Jesus' miracles were always compassionate, but they were also more than that. His miracles were signs that revealed the nature of God and the nature of life in the kingdom of God. This sign reveals that He, Jesus, is the One who can make life rich and full and joyful. It signifies also that the system represented by the ceremonial washings was inadequate. It also tells us that God must want his people to be able to celebrate things, to celebrate weddings, to celebrate with family, friends and neighbors. It tells us that joy is one of the key elements of life in the kingdom of God.

And there is something else I would like you to see here. On this occasion, Jesus did not preach. On this occasion, Jesus did not teach. On this occasion, Jesus did not ask anyone to respond to Him, to follow Him, or to believe in Him. On this occasion, Jesus simply did that which was characteristic of who He was. He just did the sign. Now then, as a result of this his glory was revealed, and his disciples began to believe. It had results He no doubt desired, but He did not pound on anybody to produce those results. Furthermore, on numerous other occasions, people came towards faith in Him, or to faith in Him, simply because of the signs He did.

"THE DRINKS ARE ON THE KINGDOM" – p. 30

If it is permissible for Christians to follow the example of Jesus, and some would say it is required, then at least two things would follow from his example here. One, sometimes, at least, it is okay to just do the stuff, to just do the Christ-like thing, without grabbing someone by the lapels and demanding a response from them. It is okay, sometimes at least, to do signs alone.

Two, it is *absolutely* required, *and* on *many* occasions, *and* by *all* Christians that we *do* the stuff, do the Christ-like thing, do things which reveal the glory of God, do things that cause the one who does not yet know God to wonder what sort of wondrous life is this that is revealed in our actions. For if we are in Christ, then our actions also, often, should reveal the glory of God. Then we should be doers of the extraordinary thing, not for manipulation's sake, but for joy's sake; not for the sake of getting another notch on our Bible, but for the sake of the joy we get from doing the extraordinary, gracious, joy-giving, Christ-like thing. Not to achieve something, though achieve something it will, but simply because it is a reflection of who we have become, of who we are.

"THE DRINKS ARE ON THE KINGDOM" – p. 31

People respond to the sign, which is the evidence of God's presence, and when they see that, they will want to pursue the God who has made it possible.

There you have it, my friends. The drinks are on the kingdom. It is we who are in Christ who are to transform the world. We do not do it alone; we do it *in Christ*, and *with others*, but we do it. You and me, we are all part of God's plan for the salvation of the world, and we do it like Jesus did: We live out a richer life, and we invite others into it.

Let's do it. Let's go make the world more like that wedding feast kingdom of God of which Jesus spoke more than once, that joy filled celebration for which Jesus gave us so much new wine.

Take a sip. It's fine. Join the party. It's grand. Invite others. We'll all have a great time, a hard time at times, maybe, but a good time. And by it we will reveal the glory of God. Go to, now. God bless you all.

"THE DRINKS ARE ON THE KINGDOM" – p. 32

"THE DRINKS ARE ON THE KINGDOM"

CHAPTER 2: LIFE IN THE KINGDOM IS A PARTY

"The kingdom of heaven may be compared to a king who gave a wedding feast for his son."
– Matthew 22:2

It Is Something Like This

It was 1954, I was eight years old. We were on a family vacation, somewhere in Wyoming, I think. I had been sick. Then I woke up one morning and I was well. I remember running across a bridge across some stream somewhere in the wilderness, and I was free. I was sick no more. I could run and play like a child again. Life in Christ is something like that.

It was 1978, give or take a year, I was reading in the gospel of Mark, chapter 2. I read about some friends who cared enough about their friend to carry him to a faith healer who was in town. That faith healer's name was Jesus. He was in a small house with many people gathered around and there was no way to get close to Him, so these guys went up on the roof, cut a hole in it, and let their friend down through that hole. How incredible. How gutsy. How wonderful. At a certain point, Jesus said to the man, "Get up, take your mat and walk."

"THE DRINKS ARE ON THE KINGDOM" – p. 34

I had read this story many times before, but now, for the first time, I heard it said to me: Get up, and walk. And that meant: God did not want me crippled! God wanted me healthy. He wanted me to walk! I had not even known that I had believed that God wanted me crippled, but now I knew that I had, *and* I knew that I believed that no more. I was set free in a way I had not been before. No physical thing changed. I was not wealthier. I was not taller. I was not thinner. Nothing in my physical circumstances had changed, but much in my spiritual circumstances had. Life in Christ is often like that.

It was 1983, or perhaps 1984. I had stopped to visit a member of my church in Highland who was then in her mid-eighties, at her summer home in Running Springs. As we chatted, she said she was upset that she could not clean her cabin as well as she wanted to because her back hurt. I suppose I expressed sympathy; I do not recall. Then it was time to go. She asked me to pray for her. Well, preachers pray for their people; so I prayed. She asked me to pray for her back; so I prayed for her back. We finished. She walked me to the door. We said goodbye. When I was half way to my car, she stopped me when she said, "Jim, my back: It's fine." Her home was the same, but her back was not, and she was glad of it. I was the same on the outside, but not on the inside. Now I knew God could use me to heal.

It was 1998, give or take a year. I went to visit a family after one of them had visited the church. Another one in the family began to come regularly to church. It was not for another two years, or so, but one day I got a letter. She said that her life previously had not been happy; she had given up all hope of ever loving. Oh, she would love her kids, but nothing more: not others, not life, and not God. Nothing had changed in the physical or material realm, but in the intervening two years, everything had changed in her life. A new world had opened up. Now she had a new joy, and new feelings, and new hope, and a new capacity to love, both people and life. She had a new life.

It was 2000, or so, a young man had a tumor in his brain. He was given a few weeks or months to live. The doctors cut out all they could, but they could not cut it all out because of where it was, and chemicals that might kill cancer cells did not work well because of where it was. The blood-brain barrier, usually a good thing was not so good this time. The next Easter, he said his doctors reported that the cancerous tissue left behind had died. It could not, and it had, and they, the doctors, called it a miracle, and so did he. Two years later, a new tumor arose. He went under the anesthetic singing "Amazing Grace" and woke up singing "The Lion Sleeps Tonight." The doctors cut what they could, but this time it was not nearly enough. He knew he had only a short while to live. He said, and more than once, that he was glad that he got the tumor that would kill him because it lead him to his church and his God.

Life in the Kingdom of God is filled with joy. Life is not always happy. Life is not always easy. Christians are not perfect. Christians make mistakes. Christians have problems. Christians worry about bills, their children, the future, their health, and their most important relationships – although far less than those who do not know Christ. Christians get sick, although, again, less than those who know not Jesus. Christians die. But we do not go into eternal darkness, but into eternal light, and we know it before we go – which makes the going a whole lot easier.

Life in the Kingdom Is Filled with Joy

I continue to explore themes suggested by the acts of Jesus at the wedding of Cana, recorded in John 2:1-11. In verse 2, it is said that "Jesus and his disciples had also

"THE DRINKS ARE ON THE KINGDOM" – p. 37

been invited to the wedding." So, Jesus was at a party, and he invited his disciples to come to. It was a wedding feast, which was the grandest celebration a Jewish couple would ever know. So this wedding feast was a very joyful celebration, and Jesus' presence at it is a sign that God approves of joy. Later in the feast, when they ran out of wine, Jesus turned one hundred and eighty gallons of water into wine. This also suggests that joy is an appropriate part of life in the kingdom of God. That was one of five points I sketched out in the first chapter, and it is *the* point I focus on here.

In Genesis 1, at the end of nearly each day of creation, God declares that what He has done is good. At the end of the sixth day, after looking over the whole of his creation, God declares that "it was very good." This understanding is in clear contrast to the beliefs of other religions, some of which have believed that creation was insignificant and others that it was positively evil.

Isaiah 55:12, speaks of God's invitation to life in him and it says, "You shall go out in joy and be led forth in peace; the mountains and the hills shall burst into song before you, and all the trees of the field will clap their hands." That speaks of joy.

"THE DRINKS ARE ON THE KINGDOM" – p. 38

In Jeremiah 29:11, God tells us, "I know the plans I have for you, plans to prosper you and not harm you, plans to give you a hope and a future." Again, this speaks good news of things that should give us joy.

When Jesus was born, angels went to shepherds in the nearby fields to tell them about his birth. They told the shepherds, and through them they also say to us: "Do not be afraid. I bring you good news of great joy that will be for all the people. Today in the town of David a Savior has been born to you: he is Christ the Lord." This is "good news." It is about something of "great joy." It is "for all the people." It tells us that someone has been born who is to be for us three things: Lord, Christ and Savior. Again, that sounds good to me.

When Jesus begins his ministry, as Mark records it in 1:15, He asks us to "believe the good news."

In Matthew 22, Jesus compares the Kingdom of Heaven to a wedding feast given by a king. He does much the same in Luke 14.

In John 10:10, He says that it is the thief who comes to steal, kill and destroy, but He has come that we may have life, and have it to the full. Abundant life sounds more like joy than misery to me.

"THE DRINKS ARE ON THE KINGDOM" – p. 39

In Philippians 4:4, Paul says that we are to rejoice all the time. Then he tells us that again in I Thessalonians 5:16.

Like it or not, understand it or not, happy with it or not, comfortable with it or not, it seems pretty clear to me that there is supposed to be a big, fat theme of joy, fulfillment, and meaning running all through this life in the kingdom of God that Jesus has come to invite us into.

In This World We Have Trouble

Now then, some say life is more or less just a vale of tears. This world is not their home. Satan owns this world. Therefore, we should not expect any joy in this world. It just might mean that we are not serving God well if we ever have any happiness. We must be doing evil if we have too much joy. We should expect rejection, persecution and misery. Indeed, our misery becomes our badge of holiness. The more miserable we are, the holier we know ourselves to be. Since Christians are not to be happy, and since, as an act of love, we want all to be Christians, then we should help others to be miserable too. The more misery we can experience and the more misery we can spread, the more holy we are and the more committed we are to the true cause of Christ! Isn't that true?

After all, In Matthew 10:38, Jesus said that anyone who did not take up his cross and follow him was not worthy of him. Then in Matthew 16:24, he says much the same thing. Doesn't that mean that we have to crucify ourselves? Do whatever is unpleasant, uncomfortable? Then in John 16:33, He told us that in this world we would have trouble. So, in this world we have trouble, and we should not expect joy, we should not look for joy, and we should be uncomfortable if we have joy. Isn't that so?

No! It is not, not in my book, and my book *is* the Bible. In addition to the scripture I cited above from Genesis 1, Isaiah 55, Jeremiah 29, Luke 2, Mark 1, Matthew 22, John 2 and John 10, Philippians 4, and I Thessalonians 5, there are over one hundred and seventy uses of "joy" in the Bible, and more than forty more of "joyful, joyfully" and such. There are over two hundreds uses of "rejoice" and another one hundred plus of "rejoicing, rejoiced, rejoiceth" and such, and still more of similar words, and still more stories which illustrate the holiness of joy.

"THE DRINKS ARE ON THE KINGDOM"

God Helps Us in Our Troubles

Yes, there is trouble in this world, but in that trouble God still moves to secure and refresh our joy. In trouble, God gives us help. There are at least three kinds of help which God brings to us when we have troubles.

I find that He gives us comfort. "Comfort, comfort my people, says your God." [Isaiah 40:1] He may not enable us to avoid all troubles, although as we follow Him that often happens. He will not always make all our problems light. But He will always make them light*er*. He will move into our circumstances and give us his presence. His presence to comfort us in grief, is a help in itself.

Jesus told us that there is a blessing for those who will mourn because God has ordained mourning as a means to get release from pain. Mourning is not a place to set up camp, but it is a place through which we must sometimes go. He tells us that He will be with us on that journey and that on the other side is comfort. "Blessed are those who mourn, for they shall be comforted." We would not mourn if we had not loved. That mourning is itself a sign of the greatness of the gift we had been given, and also a means to call in God's restorative comfort.

"THE DRINKS ARE ON THE KINGDOM" – p. 42

He will also, often, give us healing. The problem may arise, but He will enable us to get out of it. Many among us have experienced a healing that God has brought. In the New Testament, the Greek word that is translated "save" and the Greek word that is translated "heal" is the same word. Whether it is physical, emotional, spiritual, social, or even financial, God will often minister healing to us and our circumstances as we seek Him and follow Him.

I have been privileged to witness hundreds of healings of various kinds in the local church that I am a part of, and there have been thousands of healings among us. Some were of momentary pain, some were of dangerous and diagnosed illnesses, some were of deep wounds of the spirit, but He has often graced us with healing. Indeed, often our afflictions are signs that point to places that need a healing touch from the hand of God.

The third kind of help I want to mention is strength. He gives us a kind of strength to endure, to persevere, to press on. Usually, we can press on to some kind of victory, but even when we are not able to move on to a situation that looks like victory as we see it, God is still with us, and still helps us. He gives us strength by his grace, enabling us to persevere in his way and in his will. Yet while our

"THE DRINKS ARE ON THE KINGDOM" – p. 43

Lord always gives us help in trouble, we usually can experience more than that.

Jesus Turns Trouble into Triumph

There is trouble in life, but it is Jesus who turns trouble into triumph! Yes, He says, "Anyone who does not take his cross and follow me is not worthy of me," but He goes on to say, "Whoever finds his life will lose it, and whoever loses his life for my sake will find it." We do not die to things that *truly* give life. We die to things that only *claim* to give life. We may *experience* the change as a death, and indeed, it is a kind of death, but only one that leads to new life. The caterpillar may die as a caterpillar, but only to emerge as a butterfly.

For fourteen years a young man known to many of us in my church *thought* he found his life in alcohol and drugs. For two of those years, he lived in bushes just beyond a residential street. Whether he struggled back to Christ or came to Him truly for the first time, we do not need to figure out, but to Christ he came. And, while, at one point in time, it must have *seemed* like death to surrender what gave him the only source of release or happiness that he had known for many years, he came to find that real life was not in alcohol and drugs, but in the

"THE DRINKS ARE ON THE KINGDOM" – p. 44

ways of God. The results are that he has a beautiful new wife, his children back in his life, his own home for the first time ever, a good job, with great respect among those with whom he works, much happier relationships with his family than he had known for many, many years, and a peace he had never known before.

You may recall a story William Barclay tells about a working man in nineteenth century England who left off drinking and came to Christ and was chided by his co-workers for his new faith. They scoffed and laughed and asked him if he could possibly believe the story about turning water in wine. The man replied, "I don't know about turning water into wine, but in my own home, I have seen Him turn beer into furniture."

Jesus makes the same point again in Matthew 16:24-25: "Whoever wants to save his life will lose it, but whoever loses his life for me will find it." Sometimes, sometimes, it may only be in the hereafter that we will see the blessings. But even in unrelenting bad times upon this earth, still the man in Christ can know the presence of God, and *that*, that is a matter of great consequence, and in itself a real blessing. And again, it is usually the case that our death is but seeming, and we enter into new life not just by and by but now. Many of the lusts of this world are *not* means to fulfillment, but their pursuit is a sign of unfulfillment, and of a need for fulfillment which only God can meet.

Yes, Jesus said, "in this world you will have trouble," but the whole statement is this: "I have told you these things so that you may have peace. In this world you will have trouble. But take heart! I have overcome the world." This is a word to strengthen us in trouble. It is also a word to point us back to a power that can overcome the troubles of the world for Jesus can turn trouble into triumph.

Life in the Kingdom of God Is Something Like a Party

If I have made my case in your mind, then I can claim that joy *is* characteristic of life in the kingdom. I claim it is. Life in the kingdom of God should be something like a party, often and on a recurring basis. An increase of joy is the inevitable result of a real surrender to Christ, of a genuine trusting in Him. It is the relationship with Jesus Christ that enables us to see more joy and beauty in sky and sea. Christ enables us to see hope where before we had found only reason to fear. He gives us peace in place of worry. He gives us strength enough to love more than we had done before. He even enables us to let down our guard enough to receive love we had forgotten could exist. *If* joy is characteristic of life in the kingdom of God, *if* this wedding feast party is characteristic of life in the kingdom of God, then that tells us some important things about life.

Many people live life in the shadows. They have accepted a cup half empty, which, they believe, never shall be full. They have accepted defeat. They have settled for failure. They have accommodated themselves to a modest emptiness. They expect to be rejected. They may expect to be mocked, humiliated, and feel they need to smile and act as though it were a friendly joke. Many assume that *no* relationship can really be full, warm, trusting, trustworthy, open, honest, and committed. They can *never, ever* really be really real, because they can never, ever be sure it is safe. Many have accepted anger or fear as inevitable *lifetime* companions. Many dare not look too high, lest someone knock them down again. Many dare not hope too much, lest someone smash their hope again. And all this, I tell you, is a crying shame. All these, I tell you, are the very things from which Christ came to set us captives free. These things are not tokens of abundant life, and Christ came to give us that, and nothing less. Perhaps the first thing this doctrine of joy should tell us is that we should *not expect* ongoing defeat or misery.

If we are experiencing such ongoing defeat or misery, then it may be well to take it as a sign that something is wrong. Look first in ourselves to see if we have wandered from the ways of God. Look also to our spirits to see if we are full of the Holy Spirit, or if we have not let Him in very much. Yes, it may be that the evil world conspires against us, but often, even in the midst of an evil world, there is much that we can do by seeing to it that our walk is with God and that our spirits are full of His Holy Spirit.

Since we should *not* expect ongoing defeat or misery, since joy is generally possible, then we should *seek joy*. It is okay to try to find joy. After all, since the presence of joy is characteristic of the kingdom of God, then its absence is usually a sign that we are out of God's will in some way, therefore seeking joy means seeking God's will, and God's will is always something we should seek.

Again, I have seen people crippled in life by their belief that God wants them to suffer. Some think there is

"THE DRINKS ARE ON THE KINGDOM" – p. 48

simply no hope, and for lack of hope they do not seek God's joy. Others think their greatest virtue is in their claim to honor God despite the great suffering which they believe *God* has imposed upon them. But how does it honor God to call Him the author of evil? How does it honor God to blame him for all your grief? How does it honor God to believe so little in Him, to have so little faith in his ability to heal or in his desire to bless? Yes, there are times when doing the best you can when you cannot see how to do very much *is* honoring to God, but I often encounter the problem that some believe God too little, and so I tell you again, *since* joy *is* characteristic of the kingdom of God, we should *not expect* ongoing defeat or misery, and when seeming to experience it we should *seek joy* for that means seeking more clearly the very heart of God, for his heart is that you should have joy. I pray that knowing what you *can* expect, changes what you *do* expect, and that expecting better things, you do now seek it out until you find it. I pray you seek out God's joy until you have it, revel in it, and wallow in it - wallow in the joy of the Lord. I want you to raise your expectations.

   Now then, since we know that joy is characteristic of life in the kingdom, then we should *live* it and *give* it!

"THE DRINKS ARE ON THE KINGDOM" – p. 49

We should be ones who *live in* joy and who *give out* joy to others. If God has brought joy to his people, then we too should be agents of joy. Are you an agent of joy? Do people smile when they see you coming? Or do they try to look aside and avoid you? What should it be? You tell me. Well, not really: don't tell me; just tell yourself. Is your joy a sign of the presence of God's Holy Spirit within you? Of what is the state of your joy a sign? By the way, as a rule of thumb, the more you give, the more you live, and the more you live, the more you give. So go on, be giving all the joy you are living and be living all the joy you are giving. Come to the wedding feast kingdom party. Invite others. Take the party with you. Don't be a wallflower, now. Let's "party."

"THE DRINKS ARE ON THE KINGDOM" – p. 50

CHAPTER 3: THE DRINKS ARE ON THE KINGDOM

When Jesus came to the region of Caesaria Philippi, he asked his disciples, "Who do people say the Son of Man is?"

They replied, "Some say John the Baptist; others say Elijah; and still others, Jeremiah or one of the prophets."

"But what about you," he asked. "Who do you say I am?"

Simon Peter answered, "You are the Christ, the Son of the living God."

Jesus replied, "Blessed are you, Simon son of Jonah, for this was not revealed to you by man, but by my Father in heaven. And I tell you that you are Peter, and on this rock I will build my church, and the gates of Hades will not overcome it. I will give you the keys of the kingdom of heaven; whatever you bind on earth will be bound in heaven, and whatever you loose on earth will be loosed in heaven." Then he warned his disciples not to tell anyone that he was the Christ.

- Matthew 16:13-20

"THE DRINKS ARE ON THE KINGDOM"

It Was Jesus' Fault

This book is a discussion of five themes we see highlighted in the story of Jesus turning water into wine at the wedding in Cana of Galilee. While each theme is brought out by something in that story, recorded by John in 2:1-11, each theme is also highlighted by a great number of other scriptures. In this chapter, I want to focus on a passage in Matthew 16, but first let me review the basis for my argument in John 2, the wedding at Cana.

You know the story. Jesus' mother, Mary, was invited to a wedding feast. It is speculated that she was related to the couple since she apparently took responsibility for the feast going well. Jesus and his disciples were also invited. And at such an event, the whole village there would have been invited too.

Wedding feasts in their time and culture were undoubtedly the grandest celebrations that a Jewish couple would ever know in their entire lives. They were treated like a king and queen for a week. The festivities proper for everyone would have lasted more than a day, though not the whole week. Then, sometimes during this feast, they began to run out of wine.

"THE DRINKS ARE ON THE KINGDOM" – p. 53

Although there are several verses which speak of wine as a mocker, and of habitual drunkenness as a great error, there are also several places in scripture where wine is spoken of as a sign of joy. It would have been a great embarrassment to the couple for them to have run out of wine at their party. So the end of the wine would have been both a party pooper and a great humiliation. Wine here represents joy.

When it looks like they are about out of wine, Mary tells Jesus about it, obviously expecting him to do something about the problem. Jesus seemingly groans a little at her request, but He *does* respond to it. And she never doubted that He would. After He made what might have been a mild protest to her request, she simply told the servants to do whatever He told them to do, which indicates that she had confidence that Jesus *could* do what was needed, and that He *would* do it.

He tells the servants to fill up the stone water jars standing nearby. They were there for ceremonial washings, of feet when people came into the house, and of hands at meal times. The fact that John notes that these jars were there for Jewish ceremonial washings is not accidental. He is also saying that the ceremonial system which they represented is to be dealt with. Furthermore, he notes that there were six. Now everyone in their culture would have known that *seven* was the perfect number, therefore, to highlight the fact that there were six is to declare that what they represented was imperfect. Consequently, what Jesus does with them is also a sign that He is replacing the religious system they represent.

Now then, He told the servants to fill up the jars, which they did. These jars held up to one hundred, eighty gallons of water. As it is taken out to the master of the banquet, we find that it has been made into wine. So, it appears that Jesus has made about one hundred, eighty gallons of wine for a bunch of people who had already drunk all the wine they had! After all, that is why they were out, they had already drunk the large store of wine that would have been put together for this feast.

In the last chapter, I argued that Jesus' presence at a party indicated that it was okay for Christians to have joy. The fact that He also invited his disciples is further evidence of the same point. Then too the fact that He made a fairly considerable amount of wine for this party, and wine is a symbol of joy for them, is further evidence that

"THE DRINKS ARE ON THE KINGDOM" – p. 55

God wants his people to have joy. In this chapter, I argue that the same acts indicate something else too.

First, they *were* at a party! Have no doubt about that. This was a party they were at. Second, Jesus did make one hundred, eighty gallons of wine. It was surely wine, and not grape juice. (I suppose you could argue that you might lose your taste for grape juice if you drank too much, but I think the fact that people usually brought out the good stuff first argues pretty clearly that it was wine we are talking about.) And wine was a necessary element of the party to make it a joyful event for all involved. Third, and this is important, it *was* Jesus who made it. As Christians, we usually believe that we should do more or less what Jesus did, don't we? So it is important to note that it was Jesus who did this. And we usually say that *we* should do what Jesus did. If that is so, and I think it clearly is, then whatever it is that we determine is what Jesus is really doing here is something we who are Christians should also do. Isn't that so?

Now it is very important to note that this is Jesus who did it, and that also means that everything begins with Jesus. In relation to God, we do not initiate, we follow. This means that it is Jesus who brings joy. He is the author of joy. Our role is entirely subordinate to his. We must first let him bring joy to us, for us to be able to take it to others. We cannot give joy we do not have, and we get it from Jesus. That is both true and infinitely important, but now I want us to focus on our response to the joy that Jesus gives us.

Recall that we have already acknowledged that general rule that what Jesus does is what we ought to do too. So then I claim that this indicates that it is us, the Christians, who have some special obligation, or some special capacity, or both, to bring joy to others, to make life a party. In relation to others, or "the world," it is *we* who are to take the initiative to transform life. Just as it was Jesus who took initiative in response to us when we knew Him not, so also it is we who are in Christ who are to take the initiative to bring transformation to others who do not now know Jesus. Now let me see if I can find that elsewhere in scripture.

The Gates of Hell Get Beat Down

I call your attention now to another story. This is one in Matthew 16. Jesus had been telling his disciples spiritual things about the "yeast of the Pharisees," speaking in figurative language, and they do not understand. Then

"THE DRINKS ARE ON THE KINGDOM" – p. 57

He clarifies things for them more. They have gone north of the Sea of Galilee, into what would now be Lebanon, near a mountain where pagan gods were worshipped. And Jesus is going to ask them an important question: "Who am I?"

He starts by asking "Who do people say that I am?" Some said He was Elijah, who was thought to be the forerunner of the Messiah, some said He was John the Baptist returned, and others said that He was one of the major prophets. Many in those days recognized some power in Him.

That question is still in the air. Who do people say that Jesus is nowadays? Dan Brown seems to say that He was a deceiver who faked his death and resurrection. Others nowadays have said that He was a good teacher, and others that He was a good example. What things have you heard? What things have you believed?

What did Peter say? Who did Peter say that Jesus was? Peter said, *"You are the Christ, the Son of the Living God."* That was the first time that anyone had declared who Jesus was. Even so, Peter no doubt did not know all that that meant, but he knew that Jesus was the one he had been looking for. We can be like that too. At first, we may not know all that it means to draw near to Jesus, but at some point we recognize that something extraordinary is here and that it is very good and that we want it We sense that Jesus is the answer, even if we are not entirely clear on what the question is.

Who Do You Say Jesus Is?

At some point we have got to make some answer to that question: Who do we say that Jesus is? Let me put it to you directly: Who do you say that Jesus is? You see, things follow from what you say. If He is just a teacher, well, there are many teachers. If He is just a good example, well, there are a lot of fairly good examples of one thing or another. However, if He is "the Christ, the Son of the Living God," if He is the way, the truth and the life, if He is the Alpha and the Omega, the Beginning and the End, if He is the word became flesh, if He is the second person of the Triune God, if He is the very image of the invisible God, if He is the Word that was *with* and *was* God, if He is God, then what He has said is profoundly important. Then it is appropriate for us to worship Him. Then it is right for us to put our faith in Him. Then it makes sense to do what He has told us to do, whether we feel like it or not. Then we should follow Him. Then He is not a nice add-on for nice people. Then He is not just our western way of talking

"THE DRINKS ARE ON THE KINGDOM" – p. 59

about right and wrong. He is not one more thing to put in our schedule alongside work and play and family and movies and hobbies and dinning out. Then He is the basis of our understanding of *all* these other things. Then He is the mainspring that makes all these other things work as they should. Then He is God, and that makes a difference. Who do *you* say He is? Do make a note of your own answer. It is easier to keep our commitments if we are clear on what they are. So do put your own answer into words.

God Is Not Silent

There is another interesting point that Jesus makes in verse 7. He tells Peter that "flesh and blood did not reveal this to you, but my Father who is in heaven." This means that Peter's recognition of who Jesus was, was not a purely human event. It was not just a matter of human reasoning. God the Father was involved in Peter's recognition of the Messiahship of Jesus. But you see it is *never* a purely human event when *anyone* comes to a knowledge of Christ. God is in it.

Nowadays we generally sense God coming to us by means of the Holy Spirit. God's Spirit nudges us towards and confirms our new conviction that Jesus is the Christ.

"THE DRINKS ARE ON THE KINGDOM" – p. 60

Since the Holy Spirit is involved in this transaction, that tells us that we *are* in Him! And that also means that He *is* in us! And thus that He will be with us! I think there is great comfort in this: You are never alone when you recognize who Jesus truly is, not then, and, except you turn away, not ever.

Sometimes when I am feeling low, I think of I Corinthians 12:3, where Paul says that "no one can say, 'Jesus is Lord' except by the Holy Spirit." Then I say, "Jesus is Lord" once or twice to myself, or aloud, I realize I mean it, and I smile, knowing again that I am in Christ and the Holy Spirit just helped me say it. God is always in our affirmations of faith.

Maybe We Don't Know What a Rock Is Really Like

Next I would like you to see just who is this rock upon which Jesus is going to found his church. It was Peter. His name was Simon Son of Jonah. Peter is a nickname. Petros is Greek for rock, and Jesus probably called him Cephas, the Aramaic equivalent of Peter. So Jesus was calling him Rocky, like Rocky Balboa, or Rock, like Rock the wrestler. This is the rock who jumped out of the boat to walk on water and then began to sink. This is the rock who followed Jesus into the courtyards of the High

"THE DRINKS ARE ON THE KINGDOM" – p. 61

Priest and then denied Jesus three times. This is the rock who ate with Gentiles, and then refused to, and was rebuked by Paul for it. Peter was the rock here. Peter was the rock upon which Jesus would build his church. But that was made possible because he, Peter, had recognized who Jesus was. Perhaps it is the recognition of who Christ is which is the rock.

Peter sounds a lot like you and me. He got things wrong, sometimes. He rushed ahead when he might have paused. But he got the main things right. He knew that Jesus was "the Christ, the Son of the living God," and he persevered when he had messed up. He got back up and went on ahead following Jesus as best he could. Since recognition of who Jesus is was the basis for being a rock of foundation, then those who now know Jesus can be that rock too. And *we* are now the rock! We are now the foundation of Christ's church, a foundation upon which God still wishes to build.

The Church Is Us

What did Jesus say He would build upon this foundation of Peter's recognition of who He was? The Church is founded upon this rock. We are now the church, and we are the foundation upon which God intends to build. If we are not sound, then the Church does not have a sound foundation. If we crack or give way, the Church could fall. Since we are the foundation, then all that the Church is to do is dependent upon us. Oh, not just "us" in any given local congregation, but "us" throughout the world. Still, that is us, and we, us here, wherever "here" is, are important to all that God intends the Church to do.

The Church Does Not Cower

Now what is it that Jesus says this Church is going to do? He does say it in an indirect manner. He says that "the gates of *Hades* will *not* overpower it." I want you to see whose gates get overpowered. It is the gates of Hades, *not* the gates of the Church. Perhaps the better translation of *katischuo* here is not "overpower" but "prevail against." The Gates of Hell itself will not prevail against the Church which Jesus builds upon the recognition that He, Jesus, is "the Christ, the Son of the Living God," but rather this Church, of which we are a part, are to prevail against them! We beat down the Gates of Hell.

I think many Christians have an image of the Church and themselves as good civilized, Christian people in a barbarian world. We sometimes think we are something like monks in the middle ages periodically

"THE DRINKS ARE ON THE KINGDOM" – p. 63

overrun by the pagan Vikings. We huddle behind the doors of the Church because people are nicer to us there, and it is too tough for us out in the world. We huddle behind the doors of the church, hoping and praying that somehow God can keep us alive during this pagan onslaught. All we can do is hope and hide and pray that God will take us to heaven when the barbarians kill us.

That is not an image of power. That is an image of fear, and of weakness, and of powerlessness. And it is *not* the image which Jesus gives to us in Matthew 16. It is the gates of Hades that get overpowered by the Church. It is the Church that prevails against the very gates of Hell. It is *we* who are on the attack. It is *we* who beat down the gates of Hades. It is *we* who break in to Satan's territory and take back turf from him. It is *we* who, just like Jesus, break in to that territory to set the captives free. It is us who are the Church who make a difference. It is us who are the Church who move out to transform the world. It is us who are the Church who turn water-like humdrum life into wine-like new life. It is *we* who are to turn water into wine for those who are still caught up in ceremonies that will not wash. It is us who are the Church who are to bring joy to the world that knows it not.

"THE DRINKS ARE ON THE KINGDOM" – p. 64

Use Your Keys

We have enormous power. We are the ones to whom the keys to the kingdom life are given. If we do not use them to set people free, then captive they will remain. We can bind others whether we want to or not, just by not using our keys to set them free.

Everyone is looking for this freedom. Everyone is looking for freedom from fear and guilt and shame and alienation. Everyone is looking for that which will give them hope even in darkness. Everyone is looking for the celebration that they can be invited to, and feel comfortable at, and *not* feel like they are about to be tossed out at any moment. We hold the keys to that party. You have the "backstage passes." We hold the invitations. If we do not send them, no one else gets in.

The drinks are on the kingdom means that it is the *Christian* who makes the difference, who beats down the gates of Hades and who makes life a wedding feast. We *can* do more than we sometimes think. We *can* do more than we think. And, and, we are the ones who are to do it!

I want you to read a little bit from Michael Yaconelli's book *Messy Spirituality: God's Annoying Love for Imperfect People* [pp. 66-67]: "Little League baseball can be a brutal sport, especially for nine- and ten-year-olds

"THE DRINKS ARE ON THE KINGDOM" – p. 65

who compete in national tournaments. It was the area Little League championship game. The stands were packed with families of each of the players. One young man brought his mother and father, both grandparents, and three uncles and aunts to watch him play.

"The bottom of the seventh was a nail-biter. The other team was ahead by one run, the bases were loaded, two outs, and the little boy with the large family was at bat. If he made an out, the game would be over and his team would lose. If he walked or hit the ball, he would be the hero of the game.

"He swung at the first pitch and missed.

"'Strike one!' the umpire yelled.

"The families from the other team cheered, but his family cheered even louder. 'It's okay, Carl. No problem. You almost hit the ball! Now, clobber the next pitch!'

"'Strike twooo!' the umpire yelled after the next pitch.

"Pandemonium broke out. Both teams and their families were yelling back and forth at each other. Carl's family and team were encouraging him; the players and family of the defensive team were taunting. No one could hear themselves think.

"THE DRINKS ARE ON THE KINGDOM" – p. 66

"Wrinkles appeared on the nine-year-old's forehead as he waited for the next pitch. As the ball left the pitcher's hand, it became very quiet. The ball sped towards Carl. It seemed like it took forever to cross the plate, but cross the plate it did, and Carl swung with all his might.

"'Strike three! You're out!'

"Not only was Carl out, the game was over. And he was the cause of the loss.

"The winning team went crazy, their families swarmed onto the field, and everyone was dancing, laughing, cheering, and celebrating. Except Carl's team. As Carl's team walked off the field dejected, they mingled with their families and headed back to their cars in silence.

"Except for Carl.

"Carl was still standing at the plate, devastated, alone, his head down in disgrace.

"Suddenly someone yelled, 'Okay, Carl, play ball!' Startled, Carl looked up to see his family spread out over the field. Grandpa was pitching, Dad was catching, Mom was at first base, Uncle David was at second, and the rest of the family had covered the other positions.

"'Come on, Carl, pick up the bat. Grandpa's pitching.'

"THE DRINKS ARE ON THE KINGDOM" – p. 67

"Bewildered, Carl slowly picked up the bat and swung at Grandpa's first pitch. He missed, and he missed the next six pitches as well. But on the seventh pitch, determined to get a hit, Carl smacked the ball to left field. His aunt ran, picked up the ball, and threw it to first base in plenty of time, but the first baseman, Mom, must have lost the ball in the sun, because it went right through her hands into the dugout. 'Run!' Everyone yelled. As Carl was running to second, the first baseman recovered the ball and threw it. Amazingly, Uncle David was blinded by the sun as well. 'Keep running!' yelled someone, and Carl headed for third, where the throw went at least two feet over the head of the third baseman. 'Keep running, Carl!' and Carl raced for home, running as hard as he had ever run. The ball was thrown with deadly accuracy as the catcher, blocking home plate, waited to tag him out, but just as Carl reached home plate, the ball bounced in and out of the catcher's mitt, and Carl was safe!

"Before he knew what had happened, Carl found himself being carried around on Uncle David's shoulders while the rest of the family crowded around cheering Carl's name.

"THE DRINKS ARE ON THE KINGDOM" – p. 68

"One person who was watching this amazing event commented to a friend, 'I watched a little boy fall victim to a *conspiracy of grace!*'"

You, go be conspirators, conspirators of the grace of God. Greet the stranger. Invite the stranger to breakfast, or lunch or dinner, at home or to the Hilton or to Burger King. *Where* you invite them does not matter nearly so much as *that* you invite them. Invite them into life; invite them into your life; invite them into joy. Jesus does not ask you to be friendly; He asks you to be a friend. Take a moment longer to listen to a co-worker when you ask them how they are doing. Find some way to meet the need of another that they would not expect to be met. Take the initiative. Go rescue some captive from behind the very gates of Hell. Go turn water into wine. Go change someone's life. It is up to us who know Jesus to bring the joy Jesus has brought us to others. Go do it. I don't care exactly what you do to reach out and bless the other. I care that you do it. Go on now. Go do it. Go, and, in effect, turn water into wine.

"THE DRINKS ARE ON THE KINGDOM" – p. 69

CHAPTER 4: THE WHOLE VILLAGE WAS INVITED

Jesus spoke to them again in parables saying: "the kingdom of heaven is like a king who prepared a wedding banquet for his son. He sent his servants to those who had been invited to tell them to come, but they refused to come.... Then he said to his servants, "...Go to the street corners and invite to the banquet anyone you find."
– from Matthew 22:1-14

A Life Changing Moment

He was a minister and a seminary professor, and he wrote a book on preaching, but I don't recall his name and I can't find the book in my library now or I would give him proper credit. Anyway, people always wanted to ask him questions about God, but he was on vacation, and he didn't want to have to talk shop with anybody. Still, an elderly man came over to his table. He asked the man if he were a minister, the man acknowledged that he was, and then the older man began to tell his own story.

When she was young, the man's mother had not been very careful in her relationships. This story is from some years ago, and the teller was an old man then, so I put

"THE DRINKS ARE ON THE KINGDOM" – p. 70

its beginning in the 1920's, or earlier. His mother had not been very careful, and she had her first child out of wedlock – the man who was telling the tale. He grew up in a small town in the south. Everybody knew everybody's business. Everybody knew whose child he was, and folks didn't treat him kindly in those days. Being alone was the only way to avoid rebuke or ridicule.

He didn't dare go to church, well, at least not inside. He stood outside church and listened to the service. Over time, though, he got bold enough to step inside the church, but he came in late, and he made sure to leave as soon as the last hymn started.

One day, he was enjoying the hymn so much that he forgot to leave in time. The pastor had already come to the back of the church to stand by the door and greet people as they left. Well, at that point, there was nothing for him to do but to file out in the line as quickly as he could. He came to the pastor, and the pastor held his hand for a moment, looked straight into his eyes and began to speak. "Why I know you. I see the family resemblance in your face." And the young boy began to cringe outwardly and wilt inside. It was going to happen again. Just like everyone else, just like every other time, once again here was someone who was going to call him illegitimate and label him unworthy and defective. "I see the family resemblance in your face," the minister went on, "You are a child of God, and I'm glad you're here."

It was not rejection, but acceptance, and with that word, the young man's bud of faith began to blossom. He became a Christian, and indeed he later became governor of his state. His faith and his future were made possible by a church and a pastor that said, "Your real identity is as a child of God."

Who Has Access to the "Temple" Now?

In Jesus time, every good Jew knew the law of Moses. It is clear right there in Leviticus 21:17-18: "None of your descendents who has any defect may come near to offer the food of his God. No man who has any defect may come near: no man who is blind or lame or disfigured or deformed." Perhaps in Moses' time men could only see God's holiness in a man without a physical defect. But the scribes and Pharisees believed that this was a prohibition for all time and for all people and a sign that God simply had no place for such persons. But what does Jesus say? Well what did Jesus *do*?

"THE DRINKS ARE ON THE KINGDOM" – p. 72

Recall now some words we usually hear on Palm Sunday. They are in Matthew and speak of when Jesus entered Jerusalem for the last time. It is in chapter 21, beginning with verse 12: "Jesus entered the temple area and drove out all who were buying and selling there. He overturned the tables of the money changers and the benches of those selling doves. 'It is written,' he said to them, 'My house will be called a house of prayer,' but you are making it a 'den of robbers.' The blind and the lame came to him at the temple, and he healed them." Let me repeat that: "The blind and the lame came to him, and he healed them." Somehow the blind and the lame got into the Temple, and Jesus healed them. Jesus did not reject the blind and the lame. Jesus had a place for them. He healed them! That is a sign of the nature of life in the kingdom of God. God's goal is not to reject, but to transform.

Every good Jew knew that you did not talk to women who were not your relatives, certainly not in public, and certainly not to a Samaritan woman, and certainly not to a woman of ill repute, and certainly a holy man would not do that. There was a small sect of the Pharisees who were called "the bruised ones," who took pride in the fact that they not only did not talk to women in public, but they did not even look at them. They closed their eyes when they saw women approaching, then bumped into things and acquired bruises as badges of their holiness. But Jesus talked to the Samaritan women at the well in Sychar in Samaria. It is recorded in John, chapter 4. Before long, this woman, who had gone to the well at noon to escape the rejection of the townsfolk went back into town, and told the very people whose rejection she had feared only a moment before all about this man who had told her everything she had ever done. Before long, the townspeople began to believe that Jesus was the Messiah too, but it began because Jesus talked to someone who every respectable person knew you should not talk to.

Jesus was invited to dinner by a Pharisee, as Luke records it in chapter 7. "A woman who had lived a sinful life" learned that Jesus was eating there. She brought a beautiful and expensive alabaster jar of perfume, she wet Jesus' feet with her tears, dried them with her hair, kissed them, and anointed them with perfume. The Pharisee who had invited Jesus concluded that Jesus could not be a prophet or he would know who this woman was and, he believed, have nothing to do with her. But Jesus knew her,

"THE DRINKS ARE ON THE KINGDOM" – p. 74

and He praised her, and He blessed her, and He announced that her sins were forgiven.

The Jews hated the Romans for being the conquerors and occupiers they were, but Jesus ministered to the servant of a Roman centurion, and had special praise for the centurion's faith. [See Matthew 8:5-13.] Jews hated Samaritans, but Jesus made a Samaritan the hero of a parable recorded in Luke 10:25-37; it is called The Story of the Good Samaritan. Many people have thought that God could not be bothered with children, but Jesus said, "Let the little children come to me, and do not hinder them, for the kingdom of heaven belongs to such as these." [See Matthew 19:14.] Jews hated foreigners and had little regard for women, but Jesus healed the daughter of the Syro-Phoenician woman, recorded in Mark 7:24-29. By their understanding, a woman with a flow of blood should not have been out in public, let alone touch a holy man, but she touched Jesus and she was healed, as noted in Matthew 9:20-22. Time, and time, and time, and time again, Jesus ministered to those whom all the wise and holy people said should be ignored. What does that say about who gets invited into the kingdom of God?

"THE DRINKS ARE ON THE KINGDOM" – p. 75

Who Gets Invited to a Wedding Feast?

This book is an extended study of the wedding at Cana in John 2:1-11. In that story, we see that life in the kingdom of heaven should be like a party, or a big wedding feast. Since it was Jesus who made all that wine, I say that it is the Christian who should take the initiative to make life like a party for others. Today we want to ask who gets invited to the party. In Jesus time, at such a wedding, at Cana it would have been the *whole village*. Is that an example for us to follow? Who are we to invite to this wedding-feast-kingdom-of-God?

There are other places where Jesus likens the kingdom of heaven to a great banquet of a wedding feast. One of them is in Matthew 22:1-14. It is a parable about a king who has a great wedding feast for his son. Of course the king is God the Father and the son is Jesus, the Son of God. Now who gets invited? Who doesn't make it? And who gets kicked out?

The In-crowd Was Invited

First, note that the in-crowd *was* invited. They represent the Scribes and the Pharisees. They represent the leaders of the religious establishment. God had spoken to Abraham and had established a covenant with him. It was his grandson, Jacob who became Israel, he who wrestles with God. From Israel, came the nation and the twelve tribes. God had renewed his covenant with his people across the ages: the rainbow with Noah, the law with Moses, the kingship with David, the words to the great prophets, Isaiah, Jeremiah, Ezekiel and the others. No other people had such laws and such a history of divine guidance and protection. Surely no Jew doubted that they were the chosen people.

And the leaders of their religious establishment were the recognized leaders of their community. They were the custodians and guardians of the deposit of faith. They were the ones concerned for and responsible for the welfare of their community. They were the ones who earnestly sought to follow the will of God. Surely they were the ones to whom and through whom God would speak. They were the ones to decide what was sound and unsound, what was of God, and *who* was of God. Surely *they* would be invited to the kingdom of God. Surely *they* would be invited to the wedding feast for the king's Son. And they *were*. They were invited.

"THE DRINKS ARE ON THE KINGDOM" – p. 77

But They Blew It

But just like the characters in the parable that Jesus told, they did not accept the invitation. Oh, they had their excuses. They were too busy. Other matters were too pressing. Realize that in their culture, they would have accepted an initial invitation long before! The invitation they rejected was the one given when all the preparations were finally in place. But no one would reject an invitation at that point; at least no one who did not want to give great offense. Perhaps their prior attempts to follow God as they understood him were their prior acceptances, but now they rejected the invitation. Jesus gave the final invitation.

Based on what they had seen in Jesus' ministry, this new invitation obviously included an invitation to healing power, to control over the wind and the waves, to ability to make provision. Perhaps they would have accepted these things, except that they came wrapped in virtues too strange for them. Their theology was offended that Jesus would heal on the Sabbath. Perhaps Jesus had too little hate for the Romans for them. Surely Jesus must be wrong to disdain the buying and selling of animals and coins which secured their earthly wealth. Surely He was far too open to Samaritans, to women and children, and to sinners for them to ever seriously consider what He had to offer. And so they rejected it. They rejected the invitation to new life, to life in the kingdom of God which was offered them by Jesus Christ.

Note here two things: First, they *were offered* the invitation. Realize that they rejected that offer, and second, note this: If you reject the offer, you don't get it either. If you will not take what is offered, the practical effect is much the same as if you had never been offered it.

I cannot help thinking of the elder brother in the story of the prodigal son in Luke 15. The younger son wanted his inheritance, which was an insult to his father, but the father gave it. Then the young man went off to the big city and went broke, and had to slop hogs for a living. Eventually he realized that a hired hand in his father household was better off than he was, and he went home to apologize to his father and ask for the place of a hired hand. His father ran to meet him, he had the ring, sandals and robe brought, and these bespoke his place as a son of his father, and the father had the fatted calf killed to have a feast and celebrate his young son's return. But the elder brother would not rejoice.

"THE DRINKS ARE ON THE KINGDOM" – p. 79

He had been in the field working. When he came home he heard the sounds of celebration and asked what they meant. Told by a servant of his brother's return and his father's joy, the elder brother pouted. He refused to go in. The ever gracious father went out to him as well. The father tried to explain to him the need to rejoice, but the elder brother wrapped himself in his self-righteousness and his anger at his brother, and he refused to celebrate. Yet once again, if you will not go in to the party, it is the same as if you were never invited. You do not get what you will not receive.

Who is the in-crowd today? Is it the church leaders? Is it seminary professors? Is it bishops? Is it ministers? Is it ordinary folks in church? Is it us? Is it the Christians who are the in-crowd today? Is it the church members who are the in-crowd today? Are there any of us who are missing out on the party today? Are there any self-righteous ones who refuse to welcome the younger brother home today? Are our places to be taken by the folks on the street corners today? Are there those who see themselves as children of the father, but have never enjoyed being that child? Have we accepted the invitation? Are we going to the party? I hope so.

"THE DRINKS ARE ON THE KINGDOM" – p. 80

Who Got Invited Next?

Well, when the fancy people whom the king first invited did not finally accept their invitations, who got invited next? Then the king told "his servants, …Go to the street corners and invite anyone you find." It appears that God wants people to celebrate with Him. If the ones who ought to celebrate with Him won't, then He will find others who will.

In their day, I gather that Jesus meant "the people of the land," the outcasts, those poor enough to know they needed God. Jesus meant sinners, and women and children and the sick and the lame and the captive. As time unfolded, it became clear that He also meant other nations. Jesus said that more than once. People would come from afar to take the places the religious leaders would not take. And so it was to be.

Non-Pharisees got invited. Non-Jews got invited. And nowadays don't non-Christians get invited? Some may balk at that. But who else *do you invite* to come to faith in Christ? Do you just invite those who already have it? Don't you especially invite those who aren't there yet? You don't invite people to come to a party who are already at it! They are already at it! You invite those who are not there yet, don't you? So, yes, non-Christians get invited. And then can it be that messy people get invited? Yes, it can. Once again, it is not the well but the sick who have need of a physician. Who said that? I think it was somebody important. Remember Jesus invited all those messy people. If Jesus did it, isn't that some kind of evidence that we ought to do more or less the same thing? So who gets invited? *Everybody gets invited!*

But didn't Jesus throw some of them out for bad behavior? Yes, He did. Well, doesn't that mean that some will get thrown out for bad behavior? Yes, it does. Ah, ha! Then doesn't that mean that we get to throw them out? And, while we are at it, since we are going to throw them out anyway, can't we just *keep them out* now? No, and especially no. God is the judge, not us. So we are not to be too swift to throw people out. Yes, Paul will point out that church discipline may require that sometimes, but not often, and even then only to try to correct; and anyway that is not our focus at the moment. Now, as to the next part, shouldn't we *anticipate* the need and keep them out first?! No! That's exactly what the Pharisees did! We are pretty much to extend the invitation to just about everybody. Also, realize that the ones whom the king in Jesus' parable kicked out, *were invited first*. *If* they come with the wrong attitude, then they may get the axe, but first they get asked.

By the way, to any who want to try to sort of "sneak in" under some kind of false pretenses: Look, it really doesn't work. That fact was symbolized in Jesus' story by throwing the guys out, but even if people are not thrown out of the church physically, if their spirit is not right, then they are never really *in* the party anyway. People who try to mask their sins will never quite have peace anyway. We have all experienced something like that. You can be at a party, but find it all dead. You nod and smile to convince everyone else that you are having fun, but you're not, and you know it. Ultimately, for those who never get the right spirit, it gets worse. They get to keep their bitterness for ever.

Everybody Gets Invited

Who gets invited? Everybody gets invited! Insiders get invited. Outsiders get invited. God extends the invitation to all. Now, not all get in. Who does not get in? We have two groups highlighted in this story. Those who refuse to come even though they get an invitation: Hey, they don't get in. Then there are those who sort of get in, but who never get the picture, who never have the right

"THE DRINKS ARE ON THE KINGDOM" – p. 83

attitude, symbolized in Jesus' story by wearing the wrong garment, something that would have been provided for them at such a wedding in Jesus' day: They get put out at some point. God will provide us with the right spiritual garment too, but it seems we still have to be willing to put it on.

I have said that the story of the wedding at Cana illustrates several things, five of which we have been looking at. First, I said that life in the Kingdom of God should be filled with joy. Oh, life is not always a party, but there should be a big, fat streak of joy running right through it, which the wedding feast itself indicates. Second, the fact that it was Jesus who made a bunch of wine for some folks had already had a bunch, means that it is the Christians who should take the initiative to make life joyful for others. My third point, I am working on today. Who gets invited to this wedding-feast-kingdom-of-God party? Everybody gets invited. Oh, some may not accept, but then that's on them. And some may not come with the right attitude and may never get the right attitude, but then that's on them. What is on us who are in Christ is to invite. We do not want to be the ones who make up artificial barriers. We do not want to be ones who bar people from the love of

"THE DRINKS ARE ON THE KINGDOM" – p. 84

God. We do not want to be the ones who keep people from healing, hope, peace, joy, love and eternal life because *we* have some hang-up. Jesus dealt with a lot of people who were messed up by their standards. And we've got to do some of that too.

And this is not to be some tepid invitation that no self-respecting sinner would ever accept. We can't hang out with them like they have running sores and expect to do much good. This has got to be the real thing. And mind you it is an active thing, so that means that we do something like make a whole bunch of extra wine as an act of invitation sometimes, doesn't it?

Come As You Are

Well, I have got two big points I want to make in application now. The first one is this: Jesus invites *you* just as you are. Everything I said about who He hung out with in olden times - that applies now too. There is nothing in your past that can keep you from the love of God. God loves *you*. So if you have not accepted, or not fully accepted the invitation to the kingdom of God, then accept it now. Please, don't be *either* the prodigal son *or* his elder brother. Accept the invitation now.

"THE DRINKS ARE ON THE KINGDOM" – p. 85

Bring Some Others As They Are

The other thing is this. There are a whole lot of hurting people out there in that world. They all need what Jesus can give. Go see what you can do to invite them to the party. Invite them into the kingdom of God. Stretch a little. Stick your neck out a little. Move out of your comfort zone if need be. Go invite some of the people who are on the street corners of your life. Sure, maybe you invite them to church. That is good. But maybe you invite them into your life somehow, and maybe that is better, and that will lead where it needs to lead. Somehow, invite them into your life in Christ.

The whole village was invited. Mary, Jesus and his buddies came too. There has got to be some kind of message in that. What do you think it is? Let's go apply it. Thanks for considering it. Go to now, and God bless you.

"THE DRINKS ARE ON THE KINGDOM" – p. 86

"THE DRINKS ARE ON THE KINGDOM"

CHAPTER 5: THE BEST IS YET TO COME

And the master of the banquet tasted the water that had been turned into wine. He did not realize where it had come from, though the servants who had drawn the water knew. Then he called the bridegroom aside and said, "Everyone brings out the choice wine first and then the cheaper wine after the guests have had too much too drink; but you have saved the best till now."
– John 2:9-10

And we, who with unveiled faces all reflect the Lord's glory, are being transformed into his likeness with ever increasing glory, which comes from the Lord, who is the Spirit.
– II Corinthians 3:18

Save Your Fork for Dessert

You may know the story. When a certain woman felt she was near death, she told her daughter that she wanted to be buried with a dessert fork. Her daughter wondered why. Her mother told her that she had been taught as a child that during her meals she should set aside a fork for dessert. That told her that even if she did not like

"THE DRINKS ARE ON THE KINGDOM" – p. 88

the vegetables or some other thing being served, that dessert was still to come. So, throughout the meal, she knew that the best was yet to come. And now she wanted to be buried with a dessert fork as a testament that she believed that the best was yet to come.

We have been looking at the story of Jesus' turning water into wine at the wedding in Cana of Galilee. I think his participation at the wedding feast shows that it is okay for Christians to have joy. Indeed, that plus his making the extra wine, plus hundreds of other scriptures, argue that Christians should be the most joy filled people on earth. We should expect to have joy, and suspect that something is wrong when we do not have it on a regular basis.

I also argued that since it was Jesus who made the water into wine, and since we generally say that Christians should try to act like Christ, then it is the Christian who should be the one who makes life a party, who brings joy to others, who takes the initiative to transform things. We do not hide behind the doors of the church, hoping that somehow the pagan world will not destroy us, but we go out to "conquer" that pagan world and bring new and abundant life to it.

"THE DRINKS ARE ON THE KINGDOM" – p. 89

Thirdly, I pointed out that in Jesus' time, the whole village would have been invited to such a feast, and a few more besides. I take that as an indication that we, the Christians, are to extend to the whole world an invitation to this new and joy-filled life we have come to find in Jesus Christ. We do not despise, disdain or deny the sick, the troubled, the foreigner, the sinner, or any other, some opportunity to respond to Christ's call to new life.

Now I'll talk about the fourth of the five points I have highlighted in this passage. It is drawn from the comment of the master of the banquet that the bridegroom had saved the best wine for last. Eugene Peterson in *The Message Bible* puts it like this: "Everybody I know begins with their finest wines and after the guests have had their fill brings in the cheap stuff. But you've saved the best till now!" The fifth point, about the nature and value of signs, we will consider in the next chapter, but now we focus on a fourth point. What does it mean to save the best till now? I think I see a kingdom principle illustrated here. *With God, the best is always yet to come.*

"THE DRINKS ARE ON THE KINGDOM" – p. 90

God Gives You A Hope and a Future

Perhaps we need something to look forward to. Many times I have read of men of some years handling large responsibilities well and with zest, and then they retire, and shortly thereafter, they fall apart. Victor Frankl, a great psychiatrist who spent much time in the concentration camps of WW II, reported that "any attempt to restore a man's inner strength in camp had first to succeed in showing him some future goal." [Green, #679]

"Some years ago a hydroelectric dam was to be built across a valley in New England. The people in a small town in the valley were to be relocated because the town itself would be submerged when the dam was finished. During the time between the decision to build the dam and its completion, the buildings in the town, which previously were kept up nicely, fell into disrepair. Instead of being a pretty little town, it became an eyesore. Why did this happen? The answer is simple. As one resident said, 'Where there is no faith in the future, there is no work in the present.'" [Green, #678]

In Jeremiah 29:11-13, God says this to us: "For I know the plans I have for you," declares the Lord, "plans to prosper you and not to harm you, plans to give you hope

"THE DRINKS ARE ON THE KINGDOM" – p. 91

and a future. Then you will call upon me and come and pray to me, and I will listen to you. You will seek me and find me when you seek me with all your heart."

Perhaps this need of ours for a hope and a future is the grand underlying reason for God to always have something more to offer us, for the best always being just a bit further on. God has made us, and He knows what we need. But whether or not that is the reason for this principle, it is a kingdom principle that the best is yet to come. It is a principle, it is good to know that, and it brings us great benefits. I would have us look at three areas in which this principle can be seen to operate: 1) Until we come to Christ, 2) As we grow in Christ, and 3) When we go to be with Christ.

Good News

Now I want to speak of the time before we come to Christ, and of the time when we clearly do come to Him. For most of us in church, this first area is one we are sure that we know how this principle works. I hope that we do, but there may yet be some readers who have not quite got it down, and others who may benefit from hearing again.

However, first, I want to tell you that life outside of Christ is *not all* bad. Sometimes we Christians, I think,

"THE DRINKS ARE ON THE KINGDOM" – p. 92

overstate the destitution of the non-Christian in a way that does not help them see their need, but makes them mostly feel our rejection. They may think that we are not trying to convince *them* of the superiority of our position, but *ourselves* of the superiority of our position. They can feel that *we* are not so much trying to lead *them* to a joy they do not have, as to compensate ourselves psychologically for a joy *we* do *not* have!

There are many non-Christians who try to do good and do much that is good. Many work hard. Many care about others. Many are capable of being gracious at times. Many have great ability and skill and contribute much to society at large. Many have intellect as strong and knowledge as wide as the next fellow's. Furthermore, the non-Christian life can know fellowship, friendship, family and something of love. Many of their entertainments are *not* evil, and much of their life can look very much like that of a Christian neighbor. I think this is true, and I think this needs to be said for honesty's sake. For Christians to doctor the data to try to improve their "sales pitch" is shabby, and I don't think it does a darn thing good for anybody either. I also think that it is easier to hear a word from one who seems to find virtue in you than it is from

"THE DRINKS ARE ON THE KINGDOM" – p. 93

one who seems to find only fault in you, and we need to acknowledge all the virtue we can as a prelude to offering a word about something even better.

You see, despite having all the best of these virtues, I think there is very good reason to think that the non-Christian will end up in a very disagreeable place, and I do not want that for him or her. I do not say this to try to put anyone down, but I think it is true, and if it is true, then to offer help is not a mean thing. Despite having the best of these virtues, there will still, always remain a place of emptiness in the core of the soul of the one who knows not Christ.

Some of us call it a God-shaped hole. Call it what you will, but I ask the non-Christian now to acknowledge the truth here, and I think they, each, know that for all the good things with which they may fill their lives, there is something missing. I think most of us have had times when we achieved some goal and found it hollow, but non-Christians have that a whole lot. Peggy Lee spoke of it when she sang, "Is that all there is…? If that's all there is, then let's keep dancing, let's break out the booze and have a ball." But that is not all there is. And the booze does not drown out the emptiness all that well. And you're not really having a ball.

What I want to offer those who do not yet know Jesus is something that will fill that hole. That something is God. What is needed is a relationship with the living God, He who has made himself known to us in Jesus Christ. By the way, I know this may not make much sense on first hearing. But then there are many things in life which make little sense until we experience them. Isn't that so?

When Jesus spoke with Nicodemus, as recorded in John chapter 3, He told him that He had to be "born again." (Some of you reading this have no idea how much that two word phrase, "born again," makes some people bristle, how offensive they find it! And you who do bristle, know that I know that, and yet I still say you *need* to figure out what Jesus was talking about.) It means that he, and each person, needed to have a spiritual birth to have a healthy spiritual life. No birth, no life. That's not too tough to grasp. The important factor in how we experience things in life is not "the things"! It is something within us: It depends upon the life of our spirit.

"THE DRINKS ARE ON THE KINGDOM" – p. 95

Jesus began his preaching ministry by proclaiming that the kingdom of God was at hand. [Mark 1:15] I think He meant that it was right there in Him, just as it is right here now in Him. "Repent" there doesn't particularly mean "feel bad" or "grovel." It means "re-think," or "change your way of thinking." Get a new mind-set or a new world-view. "Get the picture." Then He says, believe, and that means "put your trust in," the good news. Put your trust in the good news that the kingdom of God is right here, and open to you if you will just go in.

After all, the first announcement of his birth said much the same thing. [Luke 2:10-11] The angels told the ordinary working-guy shepherds out in the fields that they had good news for them, and this good news was that there was a Savior who was born for them. There was One born who could save them, and all of us, from that emptiness at the core of our soul. Furthermore, He was both Christ, which means The Lord's Anointed, and Lord, which means God.

So, when we are not yet in Christ, it is a kingdom principle and true that the best is yet to come. Come now to Jesus. Ask Him into you heart and life. You do not have to understand fully. You just have to do it. Invite Jesus in.

"THE DRINKS ARE ON THE KINGDOM" – p. 96

However good your present life may be, and it may be very good in many ways, it will be radically changed when you invite Jesus in. "Radically" means from the root. It is something you cannot really know until you do it. So if you want to know what it is really all about, then do it. Ask Jesus Christ to be the Lord and Savior of you life. If you do it, and you mean it, then it is done, and He will be. For you, the best is yet to come. Don't settle for less than the best. Go for it.

Don't Settle for Too Little

Now some of us may think that after we come to Christ, everything is done. But that is a little like thinking that after a baby is born everything is done in that child's life! Of course over time, the baby has to learn how control bodily functions, how to walk, how to talk, how to tie shoelaces, how to use a knife and fork, how to read and write, how to get along with other children, and a whole lot more. Well the baby Christian, will need to have a similar development. He or she may also have to learn new ways to talk and new ways to control bodily functions and new ways to get along with other children of God, and so on. True, some of us grew up in fairly Christian homes, and we learned both kinds of things at more or less the same time and the need for distinctly spiritual growth may have been less obvious. But spiritual growth also has to happen for all of us along the way, somehow.

Paul wrote to the Philippians that "He who *began* a good work in you will *carry it on* to completion until the day of Christ." [Philippians 1:6] Paul's emphasis is on the presence of God to carry out the work, but it also shows that there is work to be done. It is a brand new thing when we get "born again," but it is *the beginning of a new life, not the end of it!*

Paul offers encouragement again in Philippians when he says that "it is God who works in you to will and act according to his good purpose." [Philippians 2:13] Here he is pointing out that God does two things. He *does* help you do what needs to be done, but He *does not just* help you do it, He also helps you *will* to do it! God even helps change our will, our desires, our bent to sinning, our orientation. Also, this reveals again that there is usually still more to be done.

Now in II Corinthians 3:18, Paul says several very interesting things. He has spoken of the veil which Moses put over his face after he had spoken with the people, so that they would not see God's glory fade. He likens that to

"THE DRINKS ARE ON THE KINGDOM" – p. 98

the veil which had been in the Temple in Jerusalem. This was a fabric drape several inches thick! And it was torn in two when Jesus died upon the cross. Something like that thick veil remains over the spiritual eyes of those who have not come to Christ, he points out. Now we who are in Christ, however, are not blinded by such a veil. We see God directly and we reflect God directly. (A word used there in verse 18 may be translated either "behold" or "reflect" and both meanings fit.) But then Paul talks about the things I want us to take note of.

He says that we are going on in Christ, "being transformed into his likeness with ever increasing glory." Now this means that we are now in glory, and we go on to still more glory. We are in glory, and that is no small thing. But we are also to go on to glory, and that is not something to be missed. Paul goes on to say that this is made possible by the work of the Lord who is the Holy Spirit of God. This thought should be another source of comfort as we seek to go on to greater glory.

Here is why I think this is awfully important. I see people in church sometimes settle for too little. They have abiding deep aches of the soul and they *may* have some vague hope that somehow God will take care of that when

"THE DRINKS ARE ON THE KINGDOM" – p. 99

they die, but they have *no* hope that God will or can do anything about it now. And I want to tell you that that is not the case.

I see others who seem to take pride in their pain. Although they would not state this as a belief because they know it is wrong theologically, they seem to live with the assumption that God has wronged them! They can alternate between being angry with God for his wrong to them, proud that they are really more faithful to Him than this God is to them since He has wronged them, despairing that their pains can ever be healed, and working very hard to do right in a life that gives them no joy. I tell you, do not settle for so little.

Now I do not see all my prayers answered. Furthermore, I am not sure I would trust anyone who said he did! Having said that, I want to tell you that I have seen people with long term physical ailments healed. We have heard many testimonies of that in my church. I could tell you of a woman who felt hated by her father for years, who came to feel love for him, yes, even though he had long since died, and she got greater freedom in life. I could tell you of another whose lifetime pattern of sickness ended, who talks more freely, is more confident in life, and does

"THE DRINKS ARE ON THE KINGDOM" – p. 100

things she never thought she could do, and God made this happen too. I could tell you of a man who had been molested as a child who had great hurts and difficulty in relationships, but who is now happily married and successful in life. I could tell you of surgeries cancelled, and physical symptoms, previously seen by doctors, no longer visible. I could tell of many changed lives. Sometimes the change came fairly quickly when it came, sometimes it took a fair season, although significant benefit came quickly even when there was more to come.

My point here is that I expect to grow and get more alive in Christ, both more holy and more happy! Furthermore, I think *you* should expect to grow in Christ. You should expect to get both more holy and more happy! (I do not think those are competing qualities, but they are complementary qualities. Each helps the other to be fulfilled. Holiness increases happiness, and happiness increases holiness. And we should expect more of each.) I really want to plead with you to seek more joy or peace or love of strength or whatever is missing, if something is missing. I know it does not always happen, and I do not know all the why's and wherefores, but I have seen so much happen, that I know it just about always *can* happen,

"THE DRINKS ARE ON THE KINGDOM" – p. 101

and I desperately want you to seek it. I very much hope you can hear this as a gracious word. It is not that you've *got* to get better, but that you *get* to get better! God has more glory for you, and it is good. His plans for you are "to prosper you and not to harm you, plans to give you a hope and a future." Please believe that God has plans for you and that they are plans for good. And believing that, seek God's full plan.

Even at the End of the Road

Then, at the end of our days, when we are about to go to meet the Lord, still, the best is yet to come.

The story is told that many years ago a high servant of the ruler of Baghdad was shopping in the bazaar in Baghdad when he saw the angel of death. The angel of death immediately had a strange look upon his face which the servant saw as very threatening. The servant went to his master and reported the incident, and asked if he could take a horse and go to Samara to flee this angel of death. His master gave him permission, and the servant left. But the master was angry with the angel of death for frightening his servant and he went down to the bazaar to confront him. He quickly found the angel of death and asked him what he meant by frightening his servant. The angel of death said

"THE DRINKS ARE ON THE KINGDOM" – p. 102

that he was sorry if he frightened the servant, but his look was not a threatening one; it was one of surprise. He was surprised to see the servant in Baghdad that morning when he knew that he had an appointment with him that night in Samara.

Death comes to us all, but it does not come to us all *the same*. When Paul thought of his death, he said, in Philippians 1:21, "for me to live is Christ and to die is gain." In Romans 8, he said that nothing, absolutely nothing, not even death, could separate him from the love of God which is in Christ Jesus. And John, in Revelation 21, gives us some insight into the nature of our life with Christ in the time to come. There God "will wipe every tear from their eyes. There will be no more death or mourning or crying or pain, for the old order of things has passed away."

Some approach death with great fear. Some fear the end of all that is. There will be no more to life, for there will be no more life, they believe. And all the meaning of their current life seems to be drained away by this expectation of a supposed return to nothingness. Others approach death with fear about their reward for the life they have lived. They have not lived well and they expect to

"THE DRINKS ARE ON THE KINGDOM" – p. 103

end badly. Many simply carry whatever fears or emptiness or bitterness or aches they have carried in life with them as they go to death. But for many, death is a very fearful thing.

This is not quite so for the Christian. Oh, we are an imperfect lot. Surely we grieve to lose those we love. We may feel that we have some unfinished business we leave behind and are anxious about how those matters will end. Some must contend with an end coming much too soon, and they have questions which may soon be answered but are not yet. We also do not like to suffer in the passing. Finally, I think we can say that there may yet be some fear sometimes because some desire for life has been built into us. Yet for all that, I think we go to our new life with far greater peace than those who know not Jesus.

We have a hope. More than that, we have an assurance of a new life. In many ways, we know it will be far better than what we have known here. True, there is some unease simply because we leave what we know and go to what we do not know very well.

I am pretty sure that John Wesley said something I want to quote when he was about to die though I have not found where I saw it. Lying on his deathbed, he said

"THE DRINKS ARE ON THE KINGDOM" – p. 104

something like this, "The best of all is this: The best is yet to come." And that is true. We do not know it as well as we might like, but we who are in Christ believe in his resurrection, and therefore we believe also in ours. We have found the Bible to be true as we have applied its wisdom to our lives a thousand times, and therefore, we trust what it says about that which we still do not yet know. He has gone to prepare a place for us, that where He is, we may be also. So, even though we do not fully understand, and even though we have lived long in a society which has denied all that which is called supernatural, yet we trust. We trust not only that we will live for ever with God in glory, but that that life will be good, that there will be a fulfillment and a peace and a meaning which we cannot now fully grasp, but which will then fully grasp us.

One time, "a dying man was fearful, even though he was a Christian. He expressed his feelings to his Christian doctor. The physician was silent, not knowing what to say. Just then a whining and scratching was heard at the door. When the doctor opened it, in bounded his big beautiful dog, who often went with his master when he made house calls. The dog was glad to see his master. Sensing an opportunity to comfort his troubled patient, the doctor said,

"THE DRINKS ARE ON THE KINGDOM" – p. 105

'My dog has never been in your room before, so he didn't know what it was like in here. But he knew I was in here, and that was enough. In the same way, I'm looking forward to heaven. I don't know much about it, but I know my Savior is there. And that's all I need to know." [Green, #297] That too is what we know, and all we need to know.

Always, The Best Is Yet to Come

So then, in life before Christ, in life in Christ, in life after death, the best is yet to come. While what is usually called happiness is dependent upon what happens, our joy is dependent upon what God has already done for us and upon what we know God will do. Therefore, we can have joy even in the midst of present darkness for we know that the coming light is sure. I tell you that God has more for you. *Expect more of God.* Expect to receive more of God's Spirit into your spirit, and expect to be able to call upon God's gracious power to transform your life, now and for ever. Now and for ever, the best is yet to come.

"THE DRINKS ARE ON THE KINGDOM" – p. 106

"THE DRINKS ARE ON THE KINGDOM" – p. 107

CHAPTER 6: SIGNS OF THE NATURE AND PRESENCE OF GOD

This, the first of his miraculous signs, Jesus performed at Cana in Galilee. He thus revealed his glory, and his disciples put their faith in him. – John 2:11

The Disgusted Limo Driver

In Steve Chalke's book *The Lost Message of Jesus*, he tells a story of one time when he was given a limo ride to the setting of some TV program. He had a very nice chat with the limo driver about a bunch of things, nearly all the way there. When they drew near to their destination, the driver asked him what the program he was doing was about, and in answering that, it became clear that Chalke was a Christian. To this the driver said, "Oh, no. You're not one of those, are you?" From that point on, there was *no* pleasant conversation between the driver and Chalke. The driver believed that all Christians were weird, unpleasant and disagreeable. Do Christians ever give off any signs that they are that way?

The Signs of the New Christians

I left Times-Mirror Press in January of 1978, to write the great American novel, which I never did, by the

"THE DRINKS ARE ON THE KINGDOM" – p. 108

way. God had already been working on me for some time, especially in 1977. By the end of 1978, I accepted Jesus Christ as my Lord and Savior as an adult, and I knew it was a done deal. It was not until 1981 that I began to work at the church, but I immediately got involved with visitation and a mid-week service and I was involved in other ways in the life of the church of which I became a member in 1978.

I used to visit my old friends back at the pressroom from time to time. On one of my visits in 1979 or 1980, I spoke of my new-found faith in Jesus with some of my old co-workers. One told me about a couple of guys who still worked there who reported that they had become Christians. In the eyes of my former co-workers, these new Christian guys were clannish, self-righteous, and lazy.

Now my non-Christian co-worker friends might have misread the situation, or the new Christians might have been clannish and lazy already and their new faith had not made them worse but just had not yet made them better, and they may have become model citizens later. But, assuming for the moment that this reading was more or less accurate, what kind of signs did the lives of these new Christians give out?

"THE DRINKS ARE ON THE KINGDOM" – p. 109

What Signs Do You Show?

Here is a tougher question. What kind of signs show up in your life? For a moment, think not of your own opinion, but try to think of the opinions of those who are not Christians and who know you. Do you know any non-Christians? And, by the way, if you do not know any non-Christians, how do you expect to impact the world for Christ? Now thinking of those non-Christians that you know, what would your non-Christian neighbors, co-workers, family and others say about your life if you asked them? Would they say they see in you or in your life, signs of the presence of God, the power of God, or the nature of God? If not, why not? Should they? If not, why not?

What Did Jesus' Signs Point To?

I'll set that question aside now, but I want to talk about signs. We have been talking about Jesus at the wedding at Cana, and this is the last chapter in this story. I argued that Jesus' presence at the wedding indicated that it is okay for Christians to have joy. The presence of his disciples argued that also, and his turning 180 gallons of water into wine argued that with great force. The Christian life, over all, should be filled with great joy. The kingdom

"THE DRINKS ARE ON THE KINGDOM" – p. 110

of heaven is like a wedding feast, and our lives should reflect that.

The title of the series, "The Drinks Are on the Kingdom," obviously comes from such phrases as "the drinks are on the house," and "the drinks are on me." I think these phrases are used more often in movies than in real life, but the idea is that someone extends an invitation to a whole group to have something on them, to enjoy something at their expense. To say that "the drinks are on the kingdom" is to recognize that it was God the Father who extended himself to make life possible, and it was God the Son who extended himself to make new life possible, and consequently it should be us who are in the Son who extend ourselves to make new life possible for others. We who are in Christ are the ones who should take the initiative to make life like a wedding feast for others.

My third point is that it would have been the whole village who was invited to this wedding feast, and apparently a few more besides, such as Mary, Jesus, and his disciples. From this I conclude that we also should extend the invitation to new life broadly. If someone chooses not to come, that is on them. Or, if they come and choose not to come with a right spirit, that too is on them. But if we

"THE DRINKS ARE ON THE KINGDOM" – p. 111

do not invite, we who have tasted the goodness of God, that is on us.

Sometimes it seems as if Christians fear that sin is *far* more powerful than the blood of Jesus or the presence of the Holy Spirit. If we are secure in Christ, we do not have to worry overmuch about being among sinners. Did Jesus shun them? Not at all. It is we who are in Christ who are supposed to be so contagious with our life that our life in Christ overcomes their sin. Sin is a sickness, but we have the antidote, and that is the grace of God, the love of Jesus, and power of the Holy Spirit. This is no license to *approve* sin, but it is indeed a summons to bless the sinner.

My fourth point was that, in Christ, the best is always yet to come. This is based on the fact that the master of the banquet remarked to the bridegroom that, unlike most people, he has saved the best wine for last. Here we see a kingdom principle, that with Christ, the best is always yet to come. Before we come to Christ, there is an emptiness that can only be filled by God. Once we are in Christ, we find that while we are in glory, we also get to go on to even greater glory, and all our Christian life is a growth in glory. We should expect more of God than we often do. Then, even at the end of our days, when we are about to go to be with Jesus, still, the best is yet to come, for we may look forward to something even better when we are with God in heaven.

The Presence and the Nature of God

Here I touch upon the fifth point I am drawing out of this story of the wedding at Cana. What Jesus did was a sign *of the presence and of the nature of God.* Jesus turned 180 gallons of water into wine, and that act was something extraordinary that led to belief in Him and to a greater understanding of the very nature of God.

I found sixteen uses of the words "sign" or "signs" in John. In six of these uses, there is a reference to something that Jesus did which was called a sign. This first use is in John 2:11, and refers to Jesus turning water in wine. The second such use is in John 4:54, and this refers to a time when Jesus healed the son of a royal official. The third is in John 6:2. It says that "a great crowd of people followed him because they saw the miraculous signs he had performed on the sick." The fourth sign is further on in John 6, where the story of feeding the five thousand is told, with twelve baskets of leftovers after feeding them all from the five barley loves with which they began. In 6:14, this is called "the miraculous sign that Jesus did." The fifth sign,

"THE DRINKS ARE ON THE KINGDOM" – p. 113

is in chapter 9 of John. There the story is told of the healing of a man born blind. In verse 16, this healing of eyesight is spoken of as one of a number of miraculous signs. The sixth is noted in John 12:18. The raising of Lazarus is referred to when it says, "many people, because they had heard that he had given this miraculous sign, went out to meet him."

Based upon how John calls things signs, there are other things he recorded that he might have called signs, but these are the ones he *did* call signs. There are other uses of "signs" and "signs and wonders" in the New Testament, but let us stay with John for now. What do these signs tell us?

To begin with, signs point to something. If you drive north on the 5 from San Diego, at some point you will see sign that say, "Los Angeles – 91 miles," or something like that. That tells you that a given city is a certain distance further on. You might see a sign with a curving arrow; that tells you that the road is going to curve. Or you might see a sign off the 15 that says "Menifee" and points to a turn-off, telling you that you should take that turn-off if you want to go to Menifee. If you are lost, or you are in a foreign country with not too many signs, seeing a sign can be great blessing. (I remember trying to find street names on little plaques put into the corner of buildings in Paris in 1975 to get my bearings. It was a chore to do, but a blessing to find.) It is not the destination itself, but it is powerfully helpful in helping you find your way there. A sign is not the thing it points to, but it points to something important. So what do these signs point to?

First, they point to the presence of God. Each of these signs is an indication that God is there somehow. Everyone knew that these signs showed that God was there, or at least that God was with Jesus. Nicodemus said that he knew Jesus was from God because no one could do the signs He did unless He was. The healed blind man told the questioning Pharisees the same thing: How could a sinner do the signs this man did? Obviously He was at least a prophet, the man proclaimed. Everyone knew that, except the Pharisees. The chief priests and the Pharisees were so wedded to their theology, or their personal prestige, or their power that they simply could not see the plain truth. There are people today who are still blinded by their theology or their egos who cannot acknowledge the presence of God when it is obvious. Still, signs point to the presence of God. But these signs do more than that.

"THE DRINKS ARE ON THE KINGDOM" – p. 115

Secondly, they also point out *the nature* of this God whose presence they declare. There were these six things called signs by John: 1) Turning water into wine, 2) Healing the son of a royal official, 3) Healing of a large number of people, 4) Feeding the five thousand, 5) Healing a man born blind, and 6) Raising Lazarus from the dead.

I might want to suppose that all accept that Jesus is God and so the presence of God in these signs is not something we need to establish right now, but, frankly, I hope I have some readers who do *not* now accept that idea. For them, I think it must be that if you accept the historicity of these signs, you must grant that they are a strong argument for his deity, but if you think these things mere myths then the matter is far murkier. I have seen enough of the miraculous that I have no difficulty accepting them. I hope you do also, some day. Or, if not that, then I hope that God speaks to you in some other way. But right now, however well or badly that matter is settled for the reader, I am going to consider what these signs might say about *the nature* of the God to whom they point.

What more can we learn from the acts themselves? Well, three of them are healing miracles, one of great crowds and two of individuals. That strongly indicates that

"THE DRINKS ARE ON THE KINGDOM" – p. 116

God desires us to be well, and that He has the capacity to make us well. The healing of a man born blind undercuts the then established theory that infirmities were the God-appointed punishment for sins, either of the child in the womb or of his parents. (Indeed, this healing act of Jesus might even lead us to a little humility when we are tempted to assign justice to the great affliction of another even when we see a clear connection to misconduct.) The healing of the royal official's son strengthens the argument I have made that God's blessing is intended for all people. The healing of the crowds also seems to argue that such blessings are for people in general, and not just for a select few. Over all, these signs seem to say that God can heal and that He desires his people to be well.

One sign was the miraculous feeding of the five thousand from the five barley loaves and two fish offered by a young boy there. That number probably only counts men, and we know that children were there, since a boy offered the loaves and fish, and women were probably there, so that probably means that the crowd was more like fifteen thousand altogether. This would indicate that God can make provision for us and that He desires to, and

"THE DRINKS ARE ON THE KINGDOM" – p. 117

perhaps that we should worry a bit less about provision or depend upon God a bit more for it.

The sixth sign was that of raising Lazarus from the dead. I think that John is declaring there that Jesus has power over death. Jesus can even bring back life from what appears to us to be only death. Perhaps this means that we should depend on God for life and worry a little less about death. He is also foreshadowing the message of his own resurrection: There is life after death, and Jesus has power over life and death.

So far we have three signs about healing, one about provision, and one about power over death. Clearly these are things about the nature of God's will for us that we ought to know. He wants us well, He will make provision, and He has power over life and death. Now there is one more sign I have not yet talked about.

Wine Stands for Joy

It is the first sign. This is the sign we have been talking about for six chapters. It is when Jesus was at a wedding and the folks were about to run out of wine. Jesus turned 180 gallons of water into wine. There are many other things that John said in this story and in the others, but one thing we should note here is this: Wine stands for

"THE DRINKS ARE ON THE KINGDOM" – p. 118

joy. Psalm 104:15 speaks of "wine that gladdens the heart of man." Psalm 4:7 implies that wine is a source of joy when it says that God is an even greater source of joy. It says, "You have filled my heart with greater joy than when their grain and new wine abound." And Ecclesiastes 9:7 also indicates that wine is a symbol of joy when it says, "Go, eat your food with gladness, and drink your wine with a joyful heart, for it is now that God favors what you do."

Wine stands for joy. And the turning of water into wine was the first of the miracles that Jesus did which John calls a sign. The fact that it is one at all is important, and the fact that it is the first of the signs just might be important too.

So there are four different kinds of things that God seems to be particularly concerned about, or perhaps that mankind particularly needs reassuring about: Life itself, which the raising of Lazarus addresses; Health, which the three healing signs speak to; Provision, which the feeding of the five thousand speaks to; and Joy, which turning water into wine addresses. That is pretty lofty company for joy to be with: life, health and provision. Does joy belong in such company? Is joy that important? John says it is. And God is using John here, so God says it is.

"THE DRINKS ARE ON THE KINGDOM" – p. 119

Let's go back to a verse we looked at some weeks ago, John 10:10. There Jesus says, "The thief comes only to steal and kill and destroy; I have come that they may have life, and have it to the full." If someone wants to steal your peace, or wants to be a "killjoy," or destroy your enjoyment of life, that someone is *not* of God. That person is a thief. That is what Jesus says. (I hope I do not need to point out again that I do not intend to license evil, but I speak of what leads to real joy.) The fact remains that Jesus has come that we may not *merely* survive, not *just* get by, not scrape by with white knuckles and bitter resolve, but do more than get by, indeed, we should have life to the full. Something like eating a ripe peach and letting the juice run down your cheeks, something like being at a wedding feast and having enough wine to last the whole feast through – something like that is what God wants for you. Don't sell God short. Don't trust Him too little. Expecting too little can be a kind of disbelief. Believe God for great good.

Now all that is true, and it is awfully good, and yet that is not the main point of this consideration of this sign! There are two more things I want to say about signs,

"THE DRINKS ARE ON THE KINGDOM" – p. 120

especially about what they indicate we should do in response to what Jesus did.

Some of my interest in this sign arose because I had a little conflict with someone who did not want to emphasize signs but who wanted to emphasize words. He believed that we were *not* particularly to *show* people the nature of the kingdom life, but we were to *tell* them. We were *always* to tell them. And we were *not ever not* to tell them. (Indeed, at one time, I hated to call his cell phone because if he did not answer, and he rarely did, I would have to listen to a two-minute sermonette before I could leave a message. I am afraid that he was also awfully big on theological orthodoxy and pretty dismissive of healings and changed lives as anything of value.)

Now let me say that we are indeed to tell people things about the kingdom. We are to use both precept and example. We do not only brush our teeth and hope that our children will learn to do the same by our modeling of tooth brushing. We tell them to do it. And there are a thousand other things we treat in like manner. (However, we are not always addressing children.) There are many times when things cannot really be understood unless and until they are also explained. We need language even to understand our

"THE DRINKS ARE ON THE KINGDOM" – p. 121

own experiences very well. There is a place for words, and a great place. After all, I am using words right now, and I hope they have some value! Yet having said that, I want to say that there is also a place for deeds, and more particularly for deeds which are signs, and, sometimes, even for signs alone.

You Can Lead a Horse to Water,
But You May Have To Let Him Drink on His Own

Sometimes you have to *allow* people to absorb what you have done. Sometimes you have to let people draw the right conclusion on their own, and you cannot force them to it, or you will drive them away. Sometimes you have to recognize that you are neither God nor the whole of God's plan for the world, and God may just have others to use as a part of his dealings with someone. It is not always *all* up to you. I grant you, this notion can lead some to slough off God-called duty when they should respond, but there is always the risk of getting God's call wrong, and that does not alter the fact that his call is, sometimes, to let your actions speak louder than your words, and, indeed, sometimes, His call is even to let go and let God act. You are not God, and if you insist on playing God, you may

"THE DRINKS ARE ON THE KINGDOM" – p. 122

drive some to reject God, not because they really reject God, but because they reject you!

At the wedding in Cana, so far as we know, Jesus did not preach. At the wedding in Cana, so far as we know, Jesus did not teach. At the wedding in Cana, so far as we know, He did not call for a response of faith, *but one came*! John said this: "This, the first of his miraculous signs, Jesus performed at Cana in Galilee. He thus revealed his glory, *and his disciples put their faith in him*." Sometimes, the deed alone is the thing.

Signs Do Have Consequences

In John 10:37-38, Jesus told those gathered around him in Solomon's Colonnade, "Do not believe me unless I do what my Father does. But if I do it, even though you do not believe me, believe the miracles, so that you may know and understand that the Father is in me, and I in the Father." Apparently, Jesus expected belief to follow signs. When Jesus was first calling his disciples, as recorded in Luke 5, He gave them a great catch of fish. In response to this miracle, Simon Peter said, "Go away from me, Lord; I am a sinful man!" [Luke 5:8] Here the sign led to some recognition of who Jesus was, and it led to a sense of personal sin. In Matthew 11:20-24, Jesus cries out the shame of Korazin and Bethsaida, declaring that if the miracles done in them had been done in Tyre, Sidon, or even Sodom, they would have repented long ago. So, miracles lead to repentance. From Mathew 9:8, we see that when Jesus healed a paralytic, that led to people praising God. In Acts 8:6, we find that "when the crowds heard Philip and saw the miraculous signs he did, they all paid close attention to what he said. …. So there was great joy in that city." So, miracles help people pay attention, and give them joy. And of course, we have the fact of John 2:11. This sign that Jesus did of turning water into wine led to his disciples beginning to believe in Him. *Signs have godly consequences.*

We Are to Make Signs Too

Now I have one more thing to say about deeds. *We are to do them.* Now these signs of Jesus' were good deeds, but they were not ordinary good deeds. They were super-duper good deeds. They were things that were good, and were always received as good, at least by the folks who did not have their egos pinned to a theology that just could not accept them, but they were also things that were extraordinary. They were *not* the things that everybody else did. So what does that say to us, if anything?

"THE DRINKS ARE ON THE KINGDOM" – p. 124

I think our world *is* now *somewhat* more holy than in ancient times because of the influence of Christ. To do some Christ-like things are not *as* distinctive now as they might have been two thousand years ago. Light shines brighter in great darkness, and due to the influence of Christ upon the world, the world is somewhat less dark. Caring for those in need is perhaps a more widely proclaimed virtue now than in ancient times, but there is still ample room to do the different thing, the unexpected thing, the unusually Christ-like thing. And that, I think, is something we are *all* called to. We are called to make signs pointing out the presence and the nature of God.

We too can do things to protect the life of others. We too can do things to protect the health of others. We too can do things to make provision for others. And we too can do things to sustain and increase the joy of others. And we are called to do this. After all, the drinks are on the kingdom! And we are in the kingdom; so that's us! The drinks are on us!

Ah, you might object, but Jesus did not just do extraordinary things, He did supernatural things. First of all, extraordinary things will serve pretty well on many occasions. They do also point to the presence and power of

"THE DRINKS ARE ON THE KINGDOM" – p. 125

God if they are the extraordinary things that God has directed you to do. Do not undervalue the extraordinarily gracious human thing.

Secondly, I think we can do supernatural things too, at least some of the time. If we see little that is supernatural, perhaps it is because we expect little and we pray for little. The remedy for that is not to abandon all hope of the supernatural, but to expect more and to pray for more.

Then too there have been some pretty grand things in my little church. There have been many reports over the years of tumors shrunk, lesions healed, polyps gone, lifetime patterns of sickness ended, long-term cycles of pain ended, and people who have been brought out of alcohol, drugs, immorality, anger, fear and more, and all in response to the movement of the Spirit of God.

I would like us all to try to expect a little more. I would like us to look a little more for opportunities to touch the lives of others. Sometimes the relatively ordinarily gracious thing will do. Often the extraordinarily gracious thing will do much. Sometimes, we should expect to do the truly incomprehensible thing that can only happen because God made it happen.

"THE DRINKS ARE ON THE KINGDOM" – p. 126

I began this chapter with a question about your sign language. What kinds of signs would others say they see in you? They may be blind, but that is something to consider. Then ask, what kinds of signs do you say you see in you?

A peach tree bears peaches. If you are a peach tree, you will bear peaches. Oh, there may be seasons of drought or locusts, but over all: a peach tree bears peaches. How peachy is your life?

A Christian bears Christ-like actions. A Christian bears the signs of Christ. Yes, that *might* include nail marks, but don't get too gloomy on me. If the crucifixion were without the resurrection, we wouldn't be wearing crosses, and the nail marks were not the things that John called signs. He called signs things Jesus did that restored life, restored health, made provision, and brought joy. Let's go hang up some signs. Expect to see signs in your life. Expect others to see signs in your life. Expect God to do signs through you. Sometimes, we will talk too, and perhaps often, but all the time, let's hang up some signs.

How's your sign language? I hope it is great. If it isn't, ask God to make it greater. And then go hang up some signs. Do some sign stuff. God will be with you to do it. Let's go do it. Why should we do signs? Why, after

"THE DRINKS ARE ON THE KINGDOM" – p. 127

all, the drinks are on us! The drinks are on the kingdom. So let's pour out some miraculous "drinks" that show the signs of God's presence, power and love. Let's do some sign stuff. God will be with you to do it. So let's go do it.

"THE DRINKS ARE ON THE KINGDOM" – p. 128

"THE DRINKS ARE ON THE KINGDOM" – p. 129

Small Group Study Guide For The Drinks Are on the Kingdom

Helpful Hints for Group Leaders and Participants:

Thoughts about your small group:

Size matters: Small groups usually should have at least 6 or 7 people in them, although 3 or 4 can work too. With 6 or more, there should be enough to keep the conversation flowing. Ten to 12 people in a small group is fine, but much above a dozen and there are some other problems. One of the reasons people join a small group is to have personal interaction. When you get to 14 and more, it becomes hard for everyone to have a chance to be fully included. If your group has more than 14, consider splitting into two groups.

Acceptance matters: Nobody likes getting shot down. If you think someone else is off base in their thinking, think again before you "straighten them out." If the Holy Spirit is in your group, perhaps it is not all up to you. If you are doing some scripture reading along the way, perhaps God can use the scriptures to teach without you taking on all of God's responsibility. Since your group is going to meet more than once, you may not need to correct their every error right away. If you and others are going to have an opportunity to share your understanding too, perhaps the wisdom of your position will become apparent without you directly attacking the position of another. It is also possible that your position needs some improvement too.

See here, of course folks *do* have mistaken notions all the time, and we do need to get the truth out, but it is *not all* up to us individually. And it is possible to shut people down without changing their minds at all. In such a case, they may not say anything to you, but that does not mean they agree. They may just sit silently through the rest of the session(s) until they can graciously leave and never come back. If the Holy Spirit is a gentleman, as many say, then perhaps we should be too. Consider the difference between conviction and condemnation.

Rules of the road:

Arrival time: Agreement and an understanding of the agreement are needed on some things. People often

"THE DRINKS ARE ON THE KINGDOM" – p. 131

need a specific arrival time. That is a time to get there and get settled. What people need, or want, varies. If Tom expects to start at 7:00 and Dick thinks that we get there at 7:00 and start at 7:10, Tom may get very frustrated. He may not arrive next time until 7:10, and then Dick may not want to start until 7:20. And so on. If you have a settling in time, make clear what it is. If arrival is 7:00 and start is 7:05, fine. Whatever it is, fine; just let people know. It will reduce frustration.

Faithfulness to start and stop times: It is important to be faithful to agreed upon start and stop times. Fuzzy start times can produce the frustration noted above. Fuzzy stop times present another problem. If you informally let your meeting run long because you think the discussion is particularly good, someone else may be crying inside because the time they agreed to was all their body or schedule could afford and now you are taking more from them without their approval. Their answer may be to not come the next time.

The leader should read the situation and normally start the group on closing prayer, or whatever other things make closure for your group, on time, perhaps adding that

"THE DRINKS ARE ON THE KINGDOM" – p. 132

those who wish can stay to talk about the interesting subject a little longer if need be.

No back-talk: Some groups make it a rule not to allow "back-talk," that is to say, you cannot jump in and comment upon another person's comment. In a way, I touched upon this above when I said "acceptance matters." Of course, you want to be able to have some discussion, but people need to have some freedom to share their life and thoughts without fear of reprisal. The better each member knows each other and the longer they have been together, the more you can have a flow of conversation – probably. Still, you probably need to have some version of a "no back-talk" rule in your covenant.

Confidentiality matters: Here is another matter you need to make clear early on. Generally, the rule is "what is said in the group stays in the group." Normally confidentiality does *not* include things which are harmless conversation and things which are active crimes or abuse, but one should be slow to assume that *anything* another said in the group is yours to share. Usually this is not difficult to sort out. Talk about it if you must, but I have probably talked about it too much here already!

"THE DRINKS ARE ON THE KINGDOM" – p. 133

Snacks: If you are going to have snacks, everyone needs to know what the rules are for that. Does the host/hostess plan to provide snacks for all meetings? People taking turns? Sign up? You may not have them at all, but most groups do. Just be clear on what is expected or not expected of folks.

Also, when can they get snacks? Most groups put them off until the end of the study/discussion time. That is fine, and that is the simplest. Some groups have them available during the study/discussion time. That can work too, but then folks may need to be reminded to be respectful of others' sharing: Do not make a lot of noise getting snacks and do not get up to get them at all if someone has just spilled their guts in a very personal way.

Commitment to faithful participation: Nearly always, you will want to ask people to commit to make this group a priority for the time that it is meeting. Still, someone may be sick or just cannot make it, but there needs to be some kind of commitment to faithful participation. The commitment would include group attendance, on time attendance, assigned reading, assigned praying, and possible other things necessary for the group. It is not a straightjacket, but a commitment.

"THE DRINKS ARE ON THE KINGDOM" – p. 134

Timing: Leaders, it has got to sound scary to folks to hammer them on all this at the beginning of the first meeting! Still, you will need to cover most of this before folks *leave* at the end of the first meeting. Pick out what you find are essentials. Do get group agreement to your group covenant. You should probably *not* mention anything more than "no back-talk" and "confidentiality" up front, get into the discussion, and touch upon other issues at the end of the first session.

Model leaders model answers:

One of the key goals of the leader is to get the whole group involved in the study/discussion. It is not necessary for the leader to have all the answers. Indeed, he or she should not have all the answers! He or she certainly does not straighten out everybody else's answer either, although, to be honest, he/she may do some of that, but she/he probably needs to fight against it!

One of the best things that a leader can do is to model an answer. If the first person to answer a question is open and honest, all the others will tend to be more open and honest. Yes, the leader sacrifices himself for the sake of the group. Model leaders model good answers.

"THE DRINKS ARE ON THE KINGDOM" – p. 135

The leader may go first in answering a question, especially if he wants to model an answer, but he will not go first all the time. The leader may also call upon someone whom you expect to give a good answer to start off a round of discussion.

You may use the model of going around the circle to answer a question. This has the virtue of giving each person an opportunity to speak. If you use this pattern, then you generally give people the option to pass on answering any given question. You might open the discussion to whoever wants to speak. The risk here is that some will always speak and others will never speak. If you use this pattern, then the leader should make a point to give the silent ones an opportunity to speak from time to time.

Prayer matters:

You will want to start and close your session with prayer. You will want to encourage prayer by everybody. There are different ways to do this, and you do not need to try to do everything at your first session.

I suggest that the leader start the first session with a fairly simple prayer by him or her. Depending upon your group, you may be more adventurous by the close of the first session.

One way to encourage prayer is to ask someone point blank to open or close the group in prayer. Do *not* do this unless you are pretty sure that the person you ask is comfortable with it. If you picked someone, and they do not want to pray, make it comfortable for them to say "no" and move on without making a fuss.

Another way to encourage prayer, is to announce "a season of prayer." You announce that you will open or close or some other specific person will open or close, and others are to pray as they are led in between. The risk again, if this is your only pattern, is that some will always pray and others will never pray.

Another way to encourage prayer is to ask folks to go around the circle, with each one praying as they are led. The leader announces a start person, and that persons starts. If you do this, I suggest that you give people an easy way through it. For example, tell them, "If you have nothing in particular to pray, just say 'Thank you, God,' and that is a good prayer and that lets the next one know he can pray." I have seen this work many times in groups where some

"THE DRINKS ARE ON THE KINGDOM" – p. 137

people say only "Thank you, God" for weeks and then, one time, they just blow you away with what they have to say.

A few more points:

The group discussion is a key element is this kind of study. One of our goals is not *merely* acquiring new facts about the Bible, *but coming to understand better how what the Bible says relates to our lives.* It is in the group discussion that we have a chance to make application to our lives and see what kind of sense it makes to others.

Be mindful of the time. We often tend to think that what we like is so important that we can bend the rules for our personal likes. If you have let the conversation run long, you may squeeze the prayer, or you may run over and put pressure on the ones who cannot stand to stay much longer. The group should have some general concern for time, but it is the leader who most needs to be mindful of all the elements of the program. The leader needs to move people along to whatever needs to come next, or else make a conscious decision to do otherwise for good reason.

For the purposes of estimating how a session should go, I will assume that we will have one hour and a half for a session. You will need to adjust one way or another if

"THE DRINKS ARE ON THE KINGDOM" – p. 138

your pattern is different. I will roughly assume 6 to 10 people in a group, but you can easily calculate how much time each person should take based upon your own group. I will also assume that the snack time is *not* part of this time. When I suggest the amount of time for a given segment of a session, please know that that is *only* a suggestion to give some idea of how discussion might flow. You make up your own rules as you go. After the opening prayer and report of each one's week, or "bads, sads and glads," I will usually have four to six questions. That means that your group as a whole should spend about ten to fifteen minutes on each question, or discussion block, on average. This is no straight-jacket. It is merely a means to help you move the meeting along. As you come to know your group better, you can make your own variations.

"THE DRINKS ARE ON THE KINGDOM" – p. 139

Session 1: Introduction: Getting Acquainted and Getting Started

Arrival and getting set. (About five minutes. This will not be a part of the hour and a half in future sessions. Have casual personal conversations during this time.)

Opening remarks by the leader. (Maybe three to five minutes.) Greeting people, welcoming them to the group, and giving the briefest of introductions to what the group plans to try to do, study a portion of scripture and see what lessons, if any, it may have for our lives.

Opening prayer: Let the leader offer a brief prayer for the people and the group. (The leader may omit the opening prayer the first time if this is a new group.)

Question 1: Getting acquainted: Please tell us your name; where you grew up; if you want to, tell us if you are married or single and have children or grandchildren; tell where you graduated from high school, tell us one hobby; and tell us one other personal note. (Take a minute or two per person. Maybe 10-15 minutes.)

Question 2: What one or two things are you hoping will come out of your time in this group for you? Or, if it is

"THE DRINKS ARE ON THE KINGDOM" – p. 140

applicable, tell us one or two things that you fear might come out of this group experience and which you do not want.

Read John 2:1-11. Have one person read it and the others listen, and then leave a minute or two for quiet thought. Or, have two persons read it, with a minute for thought after each person's reading.

Question 3: What are the one or two best things you ever experienced at church or thought about church? Or, if applicable, what are one or two really bad things you experienced at or thought about church?

Question 4: Have you ever experienced joy at church? In God? Do you think you should expect to have joy in Christ?

Question 5: Is your life at all like being at a wedding feast? Should it be? Have you known Christians who did something for you that was both good and undeserved? How did that make you feel?

Question 6: Where would you say your faith is at right now? Where would you like it to be? What one thought, if any, comes to you now about the wedding at Cana?

"THE DRINKS ARE ON THE KINGDOM" – p. 141

Closing: The leader should thank each for coming. Let them know that we are going to look at joy, the Christian's initiative in life, who gets invited to God, what you can expect in your future, and signs of the presence of God over the next few weeks. Tonight we have just begun.

If you have not done it before, you will need to determine the terms of your group covenant: Start times? End times? Agreement to confidentiality? Agreement on no back-talk? Or permitted responses? Commitment to faithful participation in so far as one can? Meeting place? Snacks? Other? (Maybe five or six minutes.)

Close with prayer. If the group is new to each other and/or the church, the leader may close for the group the first session. Thereafter, try to use prayer patterns that will get others involved. (Maybe five minutes.)

Homework:

If you have not already done it, read chapter one of *The Drinks Are on the Kingdom.*

Read chapter two of *The Drinks Are on the Kingdom.*

Re-read John 2:1-11.

"THE DRINKS ARE ON THE KINGDOM" – p. 142

Try to remember to pray for each member of the group, including yourself(!), once a day for this week. To facilitate that, the next page is provided for you to write or to have each one write their names. You may or may not include phone numbers too.

Group Members & Prayer List for Study:

_____

_____

_____

_____

_____

_____

"THE DRINKS ARE ON THE KINGDOM" – p. 143

Session 2: Life in the Kingdom Is a Party

Arrival time: Arrive, get settled. (Maybe a minute or two.)

Opening remarks: The leader welcomes people. He may introduce the study again, and he may remind people of the group covenant. (Maybe five minutes.)

Opening prayer: Leader may pray, or call upon another, or try to get all to pray. (Maybe 1 to 5 five minutes.)

Introductions: If there are new people, you may need to go around with introductions again. Here are some common things you might ask people to share, either this time or on a subsequent time. Do not try to use them all at one time!

    Name
    Nickname that you like
    Where you grew up
    Family information: Children? Grandchildren?
    Favorite hobby or two
    Favorite sport
    Most interesting job you ever had
    The first job you ever had
    Your most interesting vacation

"THE DRINKS ARE ON THE KINGDOM" – p. 144

> Your favorite car
> How you came to this church
> One time you felt very close to God
> One time you knew that God helped you
> (Time? Who knows? It could vary widely.)

Question 1: Share what you wish to of how your week has gone. Share things that were glad or bad or sad. How you overcame difficulties? How you got through it? What you are thankful for? Whatever is meaningful for you about your week that you wish to share, share that. (Maybe one, two or three minutes each. Maybe 10 minutes total.)

Question 2: Do you think most people associate joy with church? With God? With the Christian life? Do you? Why and/or why not?

Read: Let different ones read: Genesis 1:31, Isaiah 55:12, Jeremiah 29:11, Matthew 22:2, Luke 2:10, Mark 1:15, John 10:10, Philippians 4:4 and I Thessalonians 5:16.

Question 3: Does John 2:1-11 and the scriptures we have just read seem to say that there should be an element of joy in the Christian life? How do we have joy in church? In Christ? Should we? How should we? Can we have joy in

"THE DRINKS ARE ON THE KINGDOM" – p. 145

times of troubles? How does that work? What might that look like?

Question 4: Is there joy in your life? Would other people say there is joy in your life? Are people happy to see you come? Or are they happier to see you go? Does that say anything you need to think about?

Question 5: Assuming that we should experience joy, if we are not, how could we change that? If we are experiencing joy, do we see now someway in which that is an outgrowth of our life in Christ? What effect does it have upon your life to know that Christians should have joy? And by the way, do your dealings with other people lead them to experience more joy or less?

Closing: Leader should draw group to a close on time. Remind folks of anything that is needed for the next meeting. Lead folks into prayer. Try to get people more involved in prayer this time.

Homework:

Pray for God to show you how to have more joy. Pray for God to show you how to have joy in times of trouble, and what that might mean. Ask God what He wants you to learn about joy in the Christian life. Pray for

"THE DRINKS ARE ON THE KINGDOM" – p. 146

others in your group to have more joy, and such other prayers for them as you are led to pray.

Read chapter 3 of *The Drinks Are on the Kingdom.*

"THE DRINKS ARE ON THE KINGDOM" – p. 147

Session 3: The Drinks Are on the Kingdom.

Arrival time: Arrive and get settled. (Time?)

Opening remarks: Leader may welcome people, may thank them for coming, may remind people of confidentiality or no back-talk or other appropriate reminders, and note the kind of things to be considered at this session. (Maybe one minute, maybe five.)

Introductions: If there are new people, you may do a round of introductions again. If you wish to, see possible questions to ask in "Introductions" in Session 2. (Time?)

Opening prayer: The leader may lead in prayer, or he may delegate, or he may lead the group into something more in prayer. (Maybe 1 minute, maybe 5.)

Question 1: Sharing your week. Share your glads, sads, and bads of the week past. Share whatever is interesting to you that you are willing to share about your past week. Share any difficulty you experienced in this past week and how you overcame it. (Maybe about two minutes each. Maybe about 10 to 15 minutes.)

"THE DRINKS ARE ON THE KINGDOM" – p. 148

Read: Have someone, or several, read Matthew 16:13-20.

Question 2: Bring to mind one or two times when someone else made a positive change in your life. What did he or she do? How did it benefit you? Put down a couple of words in the space below so that you can recall your event and your memories will not be clouded as others share theirs. Then each one share their own stories.

Question 3: What did Jesus do at this wedding in Cana? How did that affect the wedding? What did wine do in that context? What does wine represent in that context? So, based on this event, what does Jesus want to do in the lives of each of us? Can you recall one time when He did something like that for you? Tell us about it.

Question 4: In the story about recognizing who Jesus was who knocked down whose walls? Who does that say is supposed to go out and take over territory from the other, Satan's followers or Jesus' followers? Based on the story about the wedding, how does Jesus do it?

Questions 5: Since it was Jesus who did it, and since we normally say that we should do what Jesus did, what does that say that we should do? Are we to bring joy to others? Are we to make a difference in the lives of others? How

"THE DRINKS ARE ON THE KINGDOM" – p. 149

can we do that? Who is supposed to do it, those who do not know Jesus or those who do? Why?

Question 6: What is one time or way that Jesus, or someone acting in Jesus name did that for you? What is one time that you did that for another? What does this aspect of this story say that we should do for others?

Closing remarks: Leader may remind folks of something or other, but this time, make it brief.

Closing prayer:

This time, do try the circle prayer, allowing each one to say "Thank you God" or "Pass" if they simply are not ready to pray out loud.

Then let each one pray asking Jesus to give him or her whatever this wine represents for him or her and to enable him or her to be able to do whatever this wine represents for him or her for others.

If anyone has not done this yet, this might be a good time to ask Jesus Christ to be your personal Lord and Savior.

Thank God for the joy, meaning and empowerment you expect Him to give you.

"THE DRINKS ARE ON THE KINGDOM" – p. 150

Homework:

Pray for each member of your group during the week.

Pray for God to show you how you can be an agent in the lives of others as Jesus was at this wedding. Ask Him to empower you to be a little bolder to do that.

Read chapters 4 of *The Drinks Are on the Kingdom*.

"THE DRINKS ARE ON THE KINGDOM" – p. 151

Session 4: The Whole Village Was Invited

Arrival time: Any?

Opening remarks: The leader, or someone he or she has designated to lead for a session, may make such opening remarks as may be needful and helpful. (Time? One minute to 5?)

Introductions: If there are new people, consider what abbreviated form of introductions you may wish to do. Look at suggestions on introductions in session 2. (Time? None? Five minutes?)

Question 1: Share what you wish about your week? Glads/bads/sads. Any new key learnings about joy or who it is who is supposed to make a difference since the study has begun? Anything interesting happening in your prayer life this week? How goes the battle? Where did you win? Lose? Regroup? (Take one to three minutes each, maybe more if something helpful to consider has been happening. Maybe 10 to 15 minutes, maybe more if appropriate.)

Question 2: Can you recall a time when you went to a place and you did not feel welcome? Can you recall a time when you went to a church and you did not feel welcome?

"THE DRINKS ARE ON THE KINGDOM" – p. 152

What happened that you did not feel welcome? How did that make you feel? How did you respond?

Read: Have one or more read Matthew 22:1-14.

Question 3: Who were the invited guests in the Matthew 22 story? What is their parallel today? Are Christians the invited guests? Do they sometimes not come to the wedding banquet? What does that mean?

Question 4: Who are the people on "the street corners"? Who are they today? Who are they for you? Are there people you really do not want in church? Should you feel that way? Talk about the real difficulties of dealing with some people, or your real feelings about some people.

Question 5: Some got tossed out in the Matthew 22 story. What does that mean? What does not having the wedding clothes on mean? How do we deal with that? Is our problem that we toss out too few, or keep out too many, or both, or neither, or something else altogether? By the way, when did they get tossed out?

Question 6: Who would have been invited to the wedding at Cana? What does that say about who we

"THE DRINKS ARE ON THE KINGDOM" – p. 153

should try to draw to Christ? What does that say about who we should "let" into "our" church?

Closing: Let the leader bring the group to a close with such reminders and words of encouragement as may be helpful.

Closing prayer:

Pray for a heart for "the whole village."

Pray for wisdom and empowerment in inviting others to the wedding feast.

Pray as you are led.

Homework:

Pray for self and all groups members each day if you possibly can.

Read chapter 5 in *The Drinks Are on the Kingdom*.

"THE DRINKS ARE ON THE KINGDOM" – p. 154

"THE DRINKS ARE ON THE KINGDOM" – p. 155

Session 5: The Best is Yet to Come.

Arrival time: (Time, any?)

Opening remarks: As may be needed.

Introductions: As may be needed. (If needed, see Introductions section in Session 2.)

Opening prayer: By now, it should probably *not* be *just* the leader praying here all the time, but do as you are led. (Time?)

Question 1: Share a bit about your week. You may share glads, bads, and sads. What has been important? What has happened in response to what you prayed last week? How have you felt close to God this past week? What have you struggled with this week? What has God told you, if anything, about inviting others to the wedding feast?
(Oh, maybe ten minutes total here.)

Read: Have one or more read John 2:9-10 and II Corinthians 3:18.

Question 2: If you can, share a story or two about something you were afraid of before you came to Christ, and how that changed once you got to know Him? All who

"THE DRINKS ARE ON THE KINGDOM"

can, share one or two stories about how something got better for you after you came to Christ.

Question 3: Those of you who have been with or in Christ for a while, can you speak of one or two ways in which your life has gotten better as you grow in Christ or continue with Him? Explain.

Question 4: Our last two discussion questions have been about ways in which we have found that life got better in Christ, and perhaps even contrary to our expectation once upon a time. In the wedding at Cana, the steward tells the bridegroom that he has saved the best for last. I think that illustrates a kingdom principle: The best is always yet to come. How can that be beneficial or helpful to people?

Question 5: How do we really look upon life after death? Be honest. Are we afraid? If so, why are we afraid, and of what? If "the best is always yet to come," what does that say about how we should look upon life after death? How can we increase our confidence in that principle operating after our death? How can we have confidence that "the best is yet to come" when we face death?

Closing: Let the leader close with such remarks as are appropriate.

"THE DRINKS ARE ON THE KINGDOM" – p. 157

Closing prayer: If she/he thinks it is possible, the leader should lead the group into individual prayers of thanksgiving for past unexpected blessings and for new blessing in the future, a new future in Christ for some, a new future in growing in Christ for some, and a new future in eternity at the right time for each of us.

Homework:

Pray for each one in your group during the week. Pray for yourself. Ask God to show you what He wants you to learn from this study. See what, if anything, God might want you to change.

Read chapter 6 of *The Drinks Are on the Kingdom.*

"THE DRINKS ARE ON THE KINGDOM" – p. 158

"THE DRINKS ARE ON THE KINGDOM" – p. 159

Session 6: Signs of the Nature and Presence of God

Arrival time: Any?

Opening remarks: Leader offers a few comments as needed.

Introductions: Not likely to be any needed. If so, do. If suggestions needed, see Introductions in Session 2.

Reading before you begin: John 2:1-11

Opening prayer: Invite God to be there to confirm what he has been teaching through the course of this time together. (Maybe 2 or 3 minutes.)

Question 1: Share your week as you are led: glads, bads, and sads. Share new learnings, key events, joys and sorrows of the week, or of the last few weeks as you have considered the themes we have studied. What good things have happened for you so far in this study? (Maybe 10 minutes.)

Question 2: By means of this sign that Jesus performed at the wedding in Cana of Galilee, Jesus "thus revealed his glory, and his disciples put their faith in him." What were Jesus' signs? What did Jesus' signs do? Think about a few

"THE DRINKS ARE ON THE KINGDOM" – p. 160

of them in the Bible that you can recall, and reflect on what they meant and achieved.

Question 3: Are Christians to be sign makers? If not, who is? If so, what kinds of signs are we to give or make?

Question 4: Are there signs of the presence of God in your life? Would your spouse say that? Your close friends? Your neighbors? Co-workers? What are one or two of those signs? And what are you saying by those signs? Think about it a minute. Be as honest as you can be.

Question 5: If "the drinks are on the kingdom," does that mean that we are to show signs of the presence and the nature of God? Do we? Should we? How might we as a church reveal more of the glory of God?

Question 6: Think this over silently. Only share if you wish to. How might you yourself reveal more of the glory of God than you do?

Closing: Let the leader say very little if the discussion has been good. Thank folks for their participation. Let people know of on-going opportunities for small group involvement. Then draw the focus back to the things brought out in the discussion for the closing prayer.

"THE DRINKS ARE ON THE KINGDOM" – p. 161

Closing prayer: Let each pray as they are led, and let the leader close the time of prayer.

"THE DRINKS ARE ON THE KINGDOM" – p. 162

"THE DRINKS ARE ON THE KINGDOM"

BIBLIOGRPAHY

Yaconelli, Michael. *Messy Spirituality: God's Annoying Love for Imperfect people* (Grand Rapids, Zondervan) 2002.

Chalke, Steve. *The Lost Message of Jesus* (Grand Rapids, Zondervan) 2003.

Green, Michael P., Ed. *Illustrations for Biblical Preaching* (Grand Rapids, Baker Book House) 1991

May, Steve. *The Story File* (Peabody, Mass., Hendrickson Publishers) 2000

McHenry, Raymond. *McHenry's Quips, Quotes & Other Notes* (Peabody, Mass., Hendrickson Publishers) 1998

Streiker, Lowell D. *An Encyclopedia of Humor* (Peabody, Mass., Hendrickson Publishers) 1998

Tan, Paul Lee. *Encyclopedia of 7700 Illustrations* (Rockville, Maryland, Assurance Publishers) 1979

"THE DRINKS ARE ON THE KINGDOM" – p. 164

About the author:

Pastor Jim Hill has been the pastor of the North Clairemont United Methodist Church in San Diego, California, for the last fifteen years. For many years, he was the President of the Evangelical Fellowship for Church Renewal in the California-Pacific Annual Conference of The United Methodist Church. From 1994 to 2000, he was President of the Board of Transforming Congregations, a national United Methodist ministry to persons in sexual brokenness. He has been published in the *American Journal of Pastoral Counseling, Pastoral Care and Counseling in Sexual Diversity*, edited by H. Newton Malony, and in *Staying the Course: Supporting the Church's Position on Homosexuality*, edited by Maxie Duunam and Newton Malony. In 1999-2000, he had a series of articles on ministry to the homeless published in the *Southern California Christian Times*. He has been a guest lecturer at UCLA, USD, and the School of Psychology at Fuller Theological Seminary.

Mr. Hill received his BA from UCLA in 1967, an MA from UCLA in 1968, and an MDiv from Fuller Theological Seminary in 1985. He was ordained in The United Methodist Church in 1984. He has been in full-time ministry since 1981.

www.ingramcontent.com/pod-product-compliance
Lightning Source LLC
LaVergne TN
LVHW011420080426
835512LV00005B/177